The Child Once Lost

A Journey To Re-Discovery

Takia Lamb

The Child Once Lost: A Journey To Rediscovery
Written by Takia Lamb

Some names and identifying characteristics have been changed and some information has been omitted for the protection of people mentioned in this book. The author is stating all events from her perspective, as she remembers it, and does not claim to hold the market on truth.

Copyright © 2016 Takia Lamb All Rights Reserved

All rights reserved. No part of this publication may be reproduced, distributed, or transmitted in any form or by any means, including photocopying, recording, or other electronic or mechanical methods, without the prior written permission of the publisher, except in the case of brief quotations embodied in critical reviews and certain other noncommercial uses permitted by copyright law.

Printed in the United States of America.
ISBN 978-0-692-81751-3

Cover Illustration by Candice McDonald
Cover Design by 4thpark

www.thechildoncelost.com

THIS BOOK IS DEDICATED TO

*The lucky ones – those who were able to find themselves,
after the times when it seemed as though all was lost.*

ACKNOWLEDGEMENTS

As always, the first honor goes to my awesome Father in heaven. God, You've been so faithful. In all of my many ups and downs, You've been patient with me, You've been kind, and You have truly demonstrated what real love looks like. When I look back at the times You've protected me, when I turned my back on You, I can't help but think of how You should have let the world have me.

You could have let every possible bad thing happen to me, but You still protected me. Even when I thought You had given up on me, You were right there with me – so open to take me back when I felt unworthy of your love. I had to accept that I did nothing to deserve Your love. Yet, the truth of the matter is that I never have. How can one earn a love like this?

Thank You for loving me.

Now, my only hope is to be everything You've planned for me to be. My mission is to hear, "Well done."

Second honor goes to my superhero husband, Rolando Lamb, Jr. I don't think I could have dreamed of someone more perfect to swoop in and pick me up off of my feet. You are a man of integrity and honor. You are a dreamer, a passionate lover, and an intense fighter. I am so in love with you and I don't tell you enough.

You've loved me when I thought I was unworthy of love. You've protected me when I felt like I couldn't protect myself. You've accepted me for all of who I am – the good, the bad, and the ugly. You are an amazing man.

You've been one of God's greatest gifts to me and an amazing demonstration of His love in the flesh. I hope, as we continue to go to war with each other, we make each other better and stronger. I pray we push each other to greatness or fail in our greatest attempt.

Thank you to my family for shaping and molding me. Thank you for telling me that I was a pretty big deal from day one. Special thanks to my siblings, Terrell, Taurice, and Arion. I would also like to mention my cousins, Charlotte, Travis, Eon, Aislinn, Tristan, Monique, Troi, and CJ, for being my very first best friends.

I have to take a step further in thanking my cousin Charlotte for being an outcast with me. We made it "cool" to be smart, spiritual, and wise beyond our years. Well, not really "cool," but I appreciate being able to go through the ups and downs with you. Our lives have always seemed to mirror each other and I'm glad we could be there to support each other through the good and the bad.

Next I have to highlight the amazing women who have helped to shape my opinion of what it means to be a strong, Black woman. First my mother, Jennifer Woods, my grandmothers, Janie Wallace and Lillie Sumpter, and my aunts, Sanasa Wallace, Tanya Sumpter, and Lisa Sumpter. Thank you all for showing me what it means to work hard and persevere. Thank you for showing me what it looks like to be unshaken. Thank you all for showing me strength in a million different ways and being go-getters.

Thank you for lending your ears to hear, and offering sound advice and words of encouragement. Special thanks to my second mother, Angela Lamb, for encouraging me as a wife and mother, and for believing in me. Your faith in me has really pushed me to be better. Your support means the world to me.

I thank God for my friends and extended family who are clearly gifts from God. Thank you to my bestie, Cheeritza St. Germain, for teaching me how to be a friend and breaking me out of my shell. Thank you for being an amazing demonstration of unconditional love. You've always made me feel like I could do no wrong, which I'm sure didn't help my ego, but it did wonders for my confidence.

Thank you to my sisters, Alicia Lopez, Ashlie Ransom, and Tatiana Benjamin, for being my "Ride and Dies", accepting me for who I am, and loving me through my darkest times. Not many people can see you go through the mud, come out a mess, clean you up and love you just the same. I hope you guys know what that means to me. It means everything, just in case you didn't.

Thank you to my life-support team, my newest group of sisters, Shakeira Wesley, Samantha Major, and Ifie Natasha Brandon for helping to mold and encourage me as a wife and mother. Shakeira, I specifically want to thank you for always being available to listen to me vent and push me back to God. Thank you for tag-teaming this motherhood thing with me. You are a life-saver. In addition, thank you all for helping me further realize my value outside of those roles and encouraging me to accomplish my dreams. You guys continue to push me to be "more."

Thank you to Tyreke Wesley, Rahqwan Major, and Xavier Brandon for lending me your wives. Thank you for supporting my husband to be a better man. Special thanks to Tyreke for your sermon on the importance of telling your story. It was definitely a large influence in getting me to this point.

To my brothers, Jonathan Stephens and Jonathan Goss, thank you for being consistent. Although, marriage and motherhood has put space between us, I can't finish my acknowledgements without giving you credit for your support and friendship. With all of my turbulent relationships, you've demonstrated true male-female friendship. Thank you for your wisdom, food, and your prayers.

Lastly, I would like to give thanks to India Nichols. I'm not sure you know, but you opened my eyes to the possibility of this book years ago. You were the first person to tell me how transformative my story was. How hopeful it was to come from such a dark place and make such a turn around. Thank you for reading my blog and encouraging me through your comments. Thank you for making me aware of my growth and sharing how it was an encouragement to you.

All of my friends and family are important to me and have had a part in making me who I am today. These are just the people that stood out to me as directly influencing me to write this book.

Thank you to everyone who has been a part of my journey.

INTRODUCTION

I began writing at a young age – from the end of elementary school into my early years in high school. I wrote stories and drew illustrations of strong female characters that overcame their life circumstances in great triumph. Those were the stories I wanted to hear.

I've always had a vivid imagination and a strong desire to tell a story to impact lives. In a sense, I've always wanted to empower women. I just never thought my own personal testimony would be the way I would do it.

As I write these words, I am further away from my "dark ages" in my mind than I am in actual time. My road to becoming lost began in 2008 and ended somewhere in 2011. Even trying to pinpoint my journey is difficult, because I've dealt with the physical challenges of being lost for a lot less time than I've dealt with the mental challenges. Even in writing this book, I've shed some tears trying to process where I went wrong.

Up until my senior year of college, I was always the good girl. I was the confident, smart, and dependable girl. Then the Christian girl, who evolved into the "Church" girl. In my opinion, those are two very different things. Honestly, I was downright "perfect" – or so I thought.

Maybe that was the issue. Maybe I was so used to being rewarded for good behavior that I couldn't motivate myself to stay "good" without external motivation. I needed someone to tell me, "You're doing a great job" or "good girl" or "I'm so proud of you." But no one owed me that.

I had to learn that there is no reward for doing the right thing, outside of actually doing the right thing. There is no reward for being responsible, other than being responsible gives people more of a reason to trust you. No one is due praise.

These are just a few of the lessons I've learned and am still learning as I process through my journey thus far. As complicated as it may seem, I was lost within myself. So lost, I couldn't recognize where I was, to find my way out.

I remember my friends telling me how they started to see my depression through the pictures I posted online. They discussed their concern amongst each other, but they didn't know how to tell me. They didn't know how to pull me out.

Now, I'm sitting at home, while my one year-old son plays on the floor. My second son is nestled safely in my womb, possibly lulled by the muffled sounds of the outside world. My husband is out visiting with his father and I am worlds away from the lost girl I once was. I am aware of who I am, still developing who I will become, and so very thankful for God's grace and patience with me.

There are many times I wonder if I had to go through the "dark places" to get here. I wholeheartedly believe those places helped me to become the person I was always meant to be, but there's still a big part of me that believes God always has an easier path for us. That's just not the path we always tend to choose.

I hope this book can be an encouragement to other women who are trying to find their way. I also hope that this book can be the warning sign to those who are on a journey to becoming lost.

Ultimately, this is my story, my thoughts, and my process. I'm not arrogant enough to believe that this is the only way, nor the best way to find oneself when lost. I'm just sharing my story in hope of changing lives. I hope to be the calm, still voice to someone that I wish someone could have been to me.

PRELUDE

Distorted Mirror

An Edited Excerpt from my blog, "The Lost Child" (2010).

The other day, I went to the mirror because I was a little sad and depressed about some things that transpired. I wanted to see if I looked like I felt. To my surprise, when I got to the mirror I did not see myself. I honestly didn't see me at all. I stared into this face and saw someone who had been crying. She was sad and broken, resembling a girl I used to know. A girl who smiled in between laughter and saved her tears for joy.

I glanced over her body and touched her face, her skin, and her hands, and cringed at the familiarity of it all. I had never been this close to a woman before. Yet, it was as if I knew her through and through. She reminded me of bubble baths and hot showers, where hours were spent indulging in childlike thoughts.

Still perplexed, I began to take all of her in. She was thin, grim, remorseful, and pained. I looked at her, feeling sorry for her, but I still didn't know why. I could not understand why I felt so close to her. So conflicted and close to her.

This is where it happened. I recognized something strange as I stared deep into her eyes. Immediately, I froze. A tremble began to rise up my spine as I inched forward to confirm what I had feared. She moved with me. I stopped. She stopped. I moved forward, she followed, and it began to sink in. That's when I looked deep into her eyes. It was me…trapped within.

It was me.

I didn't recognize myself, but it was me. This girl that I spent so long critiquing; so long I searched for her soul, but it wasn't there. It was me, but I was gone. She didn't carry me along with her on the outside like she used to. She didn't carry me to be free to speak, as I pleased. No, she caged me in as I cried out in the depths of her eyes, where she cried.

She cried because she couldn't find me anymore. She'd locked me away, convincing herself she had lost me. Now, I was lost and she couldn't pull me out. I screamed out to her insides, desperately wanting her to hear me, but she couldn't. She was deaf to her inner voice and blind to her soul. She was dead inside, yet steadily walking around the world. Doing. Seeing. Being. Gone. I was gone.

The saddest part about losing yourself is that you can't tell anyone where to find you. The saddest thing about being found is that you can't tell anyone where you'd been to keep you from going there again. I want to be found again. I want to be me again. I want to see the same smile that blossomed out of my turbulent adolescence and the same girl that triumphed over life's many stresses. So I wait. And wait. And wait to be found, as this girl carries me around.

I think I know why the caged bird sings. If for nothing else, it's to entice an ear to hear what has been captured within.

THE CONFIDENT CHILD

"In order to lose oneself, you must first know who you are."

I would imagine that if I never had a strong sense of who I was, it would be difficult to ever pinpoint being "lost." At the same time, I'm very well aware that there are many people who have always felt lost. Many of whom have always felt that they were trapped in someone else's body and in someone else's life circumstances.

These are usually people who have experienced great tragedy, acts of God, or any extreme that they identify as having a role in shaping them. We all have things that happen in life that we can't control. It's what we choose to do with those circumstances that determine who we are at the end of each and every day.

I credit my parents, family, mentors, and closest friends for shaping the foundation of my identity. They have always held a vital role in actively encouraging me and helping me to define myself. In my experience, who I believed I was had great meaning in my life. My identity played a crucial role in my accomplishments, just as much as my lack of identity was crucial role in my failures.

I believe when you absolutely know who you are and you love that person, you are less likely to give that person up.

I have always felt relatively sure of who I was. This statement in no way means that I've never struggled with self-esteem – just that I've been consistently engaged in the development of my identity.

I always felt like I didn't fit in. I had to figure out who I was, why I wasn't fitting in, and then I had to accept that reality. In my mind, different didn't mean bad.

As with many things, it started at home for me. To my family, I was Takia Ebonee Sumpter. I was smart. I was beautiful. I was strong. I was a lady. I was nice. I was Black. I had a strong sense of family. I was a good girl. These are the words that shaped my first view of myself.

I can't imagine who I would have been if I hadn't grown up hearing these affirmations. Most people I've come across who heard less positive messages really struggled with their identity. If they were told they were stupid, it was hard for them to apply themselves in school. If they were told they were bad, they did bad things for attention.

There is so much power in the words spoken over an individual's life. Especially when considering how much impact negative words can have at the beginning of a child's development of self. Of course, it's not all or nothing. Nothing is that simple. I just believe the initial words we hear shape how we define ourselves later on in life. We either spend our time affirming ourselves, as our parents have taught us, and strive to live up to the positive things we've been told or we continuously combat the negative by striving to be "more than" and/or always feeling "less than."

On the other side, one can argue that too many positive dreams projected onto children can cause resentment, rebellion, and/or never feeling good enough. You can never really know. I will just speak for what worked for me, which was positive affirmation and encouragement.

Outside of my family's encouragement, another contributor in forming my identity was seeing those spoken "attributes" confirmed in my life. I'm not sure if I made good grades because I thought I was smart or because I was. Either way, my family told me I was smart for as long as I can remember and I excelled in school for just as long.

It may have been hard to believe I was smart, if my family told me I was smart, but I didn't make the grades. There has to be some form of affirmation outside of our parent's initial praises to make these things stick. The things that I struggled with the most were the things that were not affirmed outside of my home.

Other forms of affirmation came in the form of identifying with my caregivers. As a child, I compared myself to the people that were responsible for me. My biggest role model was my mother. To this day, I think my mother is insanely gorgeous. In addition to being beautiful, she's smart and successful. Although I never had a strong desire to work in the IT field like she did, I knew I could be successful because she was. I also knew I was smart because she was.

I didn't identify with all of her characteristics as strongly, especially when it came to her beauty. I never saw myself as gorgeous, although my family always reminded me of how much I looked like her.

It just wasn't something that was affirmed for me outside of the home until much later in life.

Outside of family encouragement and affirmation, overcoming challenges or "attacks" against my identity either strengthened or crushed my beliefs about myself. This was definitely an internal struggle that marked the beginning of my journey to self-confidence.

Even with all of the self-assuredness in the world, I never felt like I fit in. Growing up, I was the only girl with two brothers. Both of my grandmothers always made a point of reminding me that I was a girl. More specifically, they reminded me of what I could or could not do because I was a girl. I was told that I couldn't play rough like the boys or I had to do the dishes, even if the boys didn't. It was infuriating.

I debated how it didn't make sense that I had to do things solely because I was a girl. Especially since a lot of the things they encouraged me to do appeared to make sense for anyone to do, i.e. cleaning, dishes, etc. I remember resenting my grandmothers for this and making a commitment to not being a "regular" girl and not letting the world define me solely based on gender stereotypes. I was perfectly fine with being female. I just didn't think being a girl meant I had to like or do girly things. I didn't like dresses and I wasn't big on how I looked or what I wore. I wasn't interested in not speaking my opinion. I was just me and I was perfectly okay with that.

Beauty was probably my biggest challenge in self-confidence. Although my family was very intentional about telling me how beautiful I was, I don't remember having that reinforced much. From my perspective, beauty looked a lot different than I did. Beautiful was light-skinned with long hair and European features. I was dark-skinned, skinny with a butt that poked out, flat-chested, had big feet, a round little nose and to top it off, I wore glasses. To add insult to injury, I didn't have the most attractive set of teeth.

My mother was dark-skinned, thin with small breasts, and average height, but like I said, I thought she was beautiful. I just couldn't see it in myself.

My solution to this growing insecurity was to become Aaliyah. Yes, the R&B singer, Aaliyah. Somehow, this seemed very rational at the time. I knew I couldn't change my skin, but I became grossly obsessed with long hair. I wanted to dress like her, I wanted my hair like her, and I wanted to sing like her. I wonder now, if I just didn't want to look like me. I didn't hate myself. I just wanted to be beautiful and I knew I wasn't.

What added fuel to the fire was feeling less desirable than my two cousins who were closest to me in age. During the summers, we spent most of our time together. One was charismatic and popular, while the other was fun and daring. Both of them began developing relationships with boys before I did. It seemed as though they were women before I was. I was late in everything. Like literally everything – from having breasts and wearing a bra to getting my period. It was a constant reminder of how I just wasn't "it".

The biggest hit to my self-confidence in this area was the lack of male attention. I won't tell all of our secrets; I'll just say summers in Boston were consumed with the corner store, random adventures across Boston, and boys, boys, boys. We met boys in every way imaginable, but my cousins were always the center of attention. I was the third wheel.

It seemed as though I was always the cute, safe one. But really, who's attracted to cute and safe?

Thankfully, my cousins were skilled in helping me to develop my tough skin. My family is the type of family that will call you out on just about any and everything. They did this about as much as they were encouraging and uplifting. I remember listening to my uncles tell stories of their childhood and picking on each other. It was all in good fun, but it could be nerve wracking, walking through the kitchen, hoping not to be the target of their next joke.

My cousins and I followed suit in poking fun at each other. There were absolutely no limits and absolutely no mercy when we all got together. A lot of it was silly kid jokes, but there were also a lot of things joked about that we were already self-conscious about.

I remember one of my cousins specifically ending all his jokes about me with, "AND you wear glasses," as if to add icing on the cake. No matter how harsh the jokes were, crying was unacceptable or you could ultimately be subjected to more scrutiny. That was just the way it was.

I think it prepared us for negativity from the outside world. I remember when I did have kids say something at school, which was a rare occurrence. I would always respond quickly and mercilessly. I remember thinking, "My cousins have worse jokes than that." This was another factor in helping me build a strong identity. No one could change who I knew I was. I knew I wasn't perfect. I didn't feel perfect, at all. Yet, somehow I realized it was okay to not be perfect. I could still be comfortable with being who I was and know I wasn't perfect.

How I got to this revelation at such a young age is difficult to explain. I believe for me it was probably a mix of logic and being extremely critical. I didn't struggle with perfection because I was always critiquing the flaws of others. When someone intimidated me, I would break down what was imperfect about them.

It wasn't a malicious thing, but it had a lot to do with self-preservation. Understanding that no one was perfect helped me to feel better about having flaws. I learned very early on that everyone has a weakness, everyone has secrets, and everyone has things they don't like about themselves. That's part of what makes us human.

The biggest lesson I learned from my cousins was to accept the ugly parts of myself, which made it hard for anyone else to tell me something I didn't already know.

It's strange coming across adults who still have significant challenges addressing their insecurities.

You can't even hint towards an area that may need improvement without them having an in-depth, internal conflict. I think we all have "blind spots," but how we are affected when those things are revealed can be an opportunity for growth or stagnation. That's up to us to decide.

Confident people learn to accept the things they don't like, just as much as they are fueled by the things they do like. It's a place of serenity. It's a delicate balance between love and acceptance.

My spiritual development was probably the final seal on my journey to self-confidence and identity. It played a vital role in putting purpose and meaning to my identity. Growing up, we were always in church, but it wasn't by choice. I don't really remember having a relationship with God, as much as I had a list of "do's" and "don'ts" to get to heaven.

Both of my grandmothers were dedicated to a small Pentecostal church in Dorchester, Massachusetts and they made sure we attended every Sunday. To be blunt, church was boring. One, we lived what felt like hours away, which meant we had to endure long rides to even longer services. Secondly, we were practically always late. Which meant we always missed the only part of church I understood – Sunday school.

This leads to my next challenge with church – I could never follow the sermons. Literally never. It was always targeted towards the adults and rightfully so – being that it was an adult church, but it wasn't appealing to children at all, which leads to the last issue of why I didn't enjoy church. We didn't really have a youth ministry and by not really, I mean we didn't have a youth ministry, as I know youth ministries to be today.

Growing up, it felt like youth ministry was more like entertainment for the adults. The leaders gave us cute things to do that we never really understood, as the adults looked on and applauded. We didn't have anyone who was really trying to connect with us. It was just a lot of information, with do's and don't's which ended with hell or heaven. You decide.

Regardless, the best times in church did happen to be Youth Sunday because we had the opportunity to get involved. We led worship, danced, and ushered. The messages were even targeted towards us, but I still didn't truly encounter God until we moved to Georgia.

When I was fourteen, my mother, siblings, grandmother, aunt, cousin, and I moved to Georgia. It was such a major change and just as exciting as it was terrifying. The exciting part was I've always enjoyed traveling and seeing new things, although, my travel up to that point had been limited to the East Coast and California. It was the furthest south I'd ever been, excluding Florida when I was too young to remember.

The terrifying part was all of the changes in such a short period of time. I was transitioning into my freshman year of high school. I had no friends, and little family. On top of that, when we arrived, we were introduced to my soon-to-be stepfather who I wasn't so sure of. My mother had dated before, but we'd never had a man come and stay. We honestly hadn't spent much time living with our mother, due to her traveling as an independent contractor since I was six. Of course, this made things even more awkward.

One of the first things that happened to me after moving – as far as developing my sense of self goes – was I became very curious about God. I guess my lack of relationships made it easier to think about something greater than the people around me.

There was also a change in my grandmother after moving. She wasn't as forceful about us attending church as she was prior to the move. I'm sure some of that had to do with her having to find a church and that we were all getting older. Regardless of her reasoning, she didn't push us anymore which was probably the biggest incentive for me, since I was the type of kid that always wanted to do the opposite of what I was "forced" to do. Especially if it didn't make sense to me. And up until that point, God made absolutely no sense at all.

This all led to a new development in my life: I actively sought out God. Which was a pretty big deal. My idea of church and God was changing from being my grandmother's thing, to something I could participate in. This also changed my church experience. Although, I still wasn't involved in a youth ministry, I was actually starting to understand the messages.

I think a large part of what made God intriguing was my grandmothers' dedication. As a young child, I remember watching both of them practicing their faith with such hypnotizing devotion. They never missed church, attended every event, gave tithes and offering, and prayed religiously. Watching them pray had to be the most impactful act of faith for my younger self. Every night, before bed, my grandmothers would get on their knees and whisper to God. Then they would wake up before everyone else in the house, pray, and begin their day.

I could never hear their prayers, but they were completely entranced in those moments. They weren't troubled by the noise my brothers and I made or whatever else was going on. It was almost like they weren't even there. As a child, I didn't understand.

As a teenager, it became something I needed to understand. What could cause such devotion, that people would dedicate their lives to it, day-in and day-out? What could captivate anyone for that long, unless it was just that captivating?

The day I experienced God for the first time was December 31, 2001. We were at the watch night service at a church I can't remember the name of and the preacher made a call for salvation. I remember feeling strange, almost nervous, and felt a strong pull to go. I was so anxious. I had heard stories about encounters with God, but I didn't know God. I didn't know what it would really mean to be saved.

I grew up thinking it meant not breaking God's rules and I honestly didn't know if I was capable of that. I didn't have any examples of young Christians, so the assumption was that I would have to be transformed into my grandmothers, and I definitely wasn't sure I could do that. I wanted to know God, but I wasn't sure it was something I was ready for.

When I finally got the courage to walk up to the altar, it was at the very end of the prayer call. It was so late, I didn't get prayed for in the front like everyone else. They pulled me to the side while the pastor finished speaking. I remember a woman praying for me. I don't remember anything she said, except that she described the feeling in the pit of my stomach and explained that it was God trying to get my attention. That was when I knew I wanted to give my life to Christ. I still didn't know what that meant. I just knew it was something I needed to know.

I was baptized on January 1, 2002. It was the most supernatural thing I had ever experienced at the time. I was dipped in a pool, surrounded by strangers, and when I came up, I felt brand new. I'm sure it sounds cliché, but something about the whole experience made me feel lighter. Like a whole new world opened up to me.

After getting saved, I had no idea what to do. I remember thinking I needed to change my behavior, but I wasn't necessarily a "bad" kid. So, it was difficult to decide what my life needed to look like. I settled on a need to stop cursing, to go to church, and read my Bible.

One thing I realized that changed almost immediately after I got saved was the adults in my life began to see me differently. They actually began to seek my advice. I thought it was the strangest thing. It was like I graduated into another level of maturity.

The earliest instance of this new phenomenon was my grandmother asking me whether she should make my brothers go to church. I remember telling her I didn't think forcing someone to attend church would change them. A relationship with God was a personal choice they needed to make when they were ready.

Surprisingly enough, she agreed. She knew it was true, but I could tell it was a difficult decision for her. She was genuinely concerned for their well-being. It was even more surprising that I understood her dilemma. But the truth is, you can lead a horse to water but you can't make it drink. That was something I struggled with early in my walk, as with many Christians. I wanted to share God with everyone, but everyone wasn't necessarily in a place where they wanted to receive God. Many people have already made their decision about God before they've even tried to get to know Him.

Regardless, the relationship is something that needs to take place between God and that person. The best thing we can do as Christians is to live out our faith the best way we know how and be ready to share when the interest arises.

Ironically, despite my grandmothers' dedication drawing me to God, my family members had a limited role in my spiritual development. One of the most influential people in helping me develop my spiritual foundation was my first, male best friend. I met him shortly after becoming best friends with my best friend-forever, Cheeritza, or Za. Although, I've called her a lot of nicknames she'd probably rather I not mention in this book.

We met our male best friend, Desmond, in our sophomore year geometry class. He was very quiet and to himself, but that didn't stop us from "encouraging" him to talk. When we did succeed in getting him to talk, he was not only funny, but he was Christian. Like, a serious Christian. At the time, I didn't know any people my age that were really serious about living a Christian life. Nor did I know many people who could tell me how to do it and more importantly, show me why.

As we continued to provoke him to speak, he talked a lot about God. One of the biggest things I took from those talks was the importance of reading and knowing the Bible for yourself. His response to most of my questions was, "it's all right here" as he pointed to the Bible. He was adamant about going to the source for all the answers.

It was life changing.

As a child, I thought the preacher was supposed to give you all the answers. They were charged with telling you how to live, or at least that appeared to be most people's reality. I didn't know I could access God without a middleman. I did know that I didn't want to wait until Sunday to learn more about God. I wanted the access to God that the people in the Bible had. That's what Desmond helped me begin to understand.

Outside of my spiritual development, both of my best friends helped to shape my understanding of what it meant to be in a healthy relationship. We spent lots of time together. We talked on the phone all night. We encouraged each other and shared our dreams. As confident as I would say I was growing up, I was at the height of my self-confidence with friends like them around me.

I'll never forget one of the first times Za and I ever spoke. About a minute into the conversation, she said something like, "Wow, your toes are dark." I remember staring at her and thinking, "Why would she say that?" Yet, in sum, that's Za. She always says the first thing on her mind. She's bubbly, charismatic and supportive. These are all things I grew to admire about her. She's unapologetically her and loves her friends unapologetically.

It wasn't something I was used to. I accepted me, but I don't know if I was as bold as she was with it. With all of the self-evaluation in the world, I didn't know how others felt about me and it was something I wondered at times. Za made me feel like it was not only okay being me, but it was okay being me around other people. She made me realize I was kind of a big deal.

They both also had a big hand in building my self-confidence. And for the latter part of high school into college, Desmond and I dated.

At the time, I believed it was an act of friendship. Recently, it occurred to me that he might have actually liked me for longer than I was aware of, which again speaks to me feeling relatively undesirable physically. Even when boys did like me, I could never take them seriously.

I remember telling Desmond during one of our late night conversations that I was tired of being single. At sixteen, I felt I was ready for a serious relationship. So, he suggested, "Well, why don't I just be your boyfriend until you find someone better?"

It was a simple suggestion and when I stopped and thought about it, it seemed like a pretty good idea. I followed up by asking, "So, what would change?" He told me nothing would change. We would simply be boyfriend and girlfriend. Not complicated at all, right? So, I agreed.

When I told Za, she was shocked, but very supportive. We dated for three and a half years and I was blessed to have that as my first romantic experience. It was a great boost to my self-confidence. I finally felt like my beauty was validated and life was complete.

Of course, everything wasn't perfect, but it was amazing for confirming: (1) I am desirable, (2) I am pretty, (3) I am smart, and (4) a successful relationship, for me at least, starts with friendship. Additionally, Za always raved about me. It was a wonderful finish on molding and shaping me into my younger self.

When I look back on the development of my self-esteem, I feel like God hid me away at times. In those moments of hiding, though, I felt alone. Now, in retrospect, I feel like He was positioning me for something more. Even in my relationship with Desmond – for a while I thought, "He's just being a nice friend." That could have been his original intent, but it was difficult to embrace the idea that he wanted to be with me because he liked me.

Freshman year at Spelman College was a whole new ballgame. It was filled with new people, new experiences, and lots and lots of new challenges.

This meant the beginning of fine-tuning myself, which also meant a lot of the old things in my life would struggle to stay relevant.

Initially, I was assigned to a room with two roommates, one from San Diego and one from Atlanta. I spent most of my time with my roommate from San Diego, mainly because we clicked immediately and seemed to have a lot in common. We initially bonded over our desire to get involved in the Christian activities around campus.

I think another major factor in us initially bonding was that we were both in a completely new environment. Our other roommate was very familiar with the school and had lots of established relationships. One thing I remain grateful for is that I was blessed with two amazing roommates that I love. We became like sisters very quickly, which was a lot of what made my freshman year so impactful.

My first major struggle in college was between Desmond and I. Before then, we had never been apart for long, but we suddenly fell into a long-distance relationship. He moved to Detroit for work right before I moved into Atlanta to start school.

When I got to school, it was really tough for me to balance all of the newness and be as available to him as I had been. That really put a major strain on our relationship, as I'd been consistently available for our entire friendship. We officially parted ways my first winter break in college after a visit to Detroit. Although initially, it was a break, it quickly turned into a break-up. I definitely don't recommend trying to manage a long-distance relationship at the start of college.

Even though I loved him immensely, I was so eager for freedom. I'm not sure I'd ever felt that free before and it was intoxicating. I think he knew that, which might have been a large part of his frustration. I was completely oblivious.

After my break-up, my San Diego roommate and I became even more inseparable. We attended Christian plays and parties. We visited different churches and joined a campus youth ministry called Christian Youth Fellowship. We were pretty dedicated to being engulfed in God. We even served on the usher board for Morehouse's King Chapel, which is humorous when I think about it, because I'm not sure that was actually a thing before us. Either way, I think we officially achieved "Church Girl" status – all action and little substance – for me at least. Which leads us to the "other side" of freshman year.

College was definitely a time of exploration. For the first time in my life, I experienced the club, twerking, and casual dating, which also resulted in a few dangerous, close encounters.

One night, during "Parking Lot Pimping", an Atlanta University Center (AUC) term for all of the boo-loving that happened in the parking lot outside of Spelman's pearly gates, a guy propositioned me for my number. I remember my roommate telling me the guy was really cute and validating that I should give him my number. We exchanged numbers and that was that. That next weekend, we were bored and the "Parking Lot Guy" texted me, asking me to come over. I told my roommate and she was like, "Let's go!" So, we went.

As soon as we heard the car doors close behind us, we knew we were in a bad situation. We rode in the back of an all-white Charger, speeding through red lights with music blasting through the speakers. Neither of the two strange men we got in the car with said a word to us and we had no idea where we were going. My roommate and I just gave each other a look, grabbed hands, and prayed.

Some of you might be reading this thinking, "Whaaat?" Oh, but it gets worse. We finally got to where we were going and it was a random motel somewhere in downtown Atlanta. It was the middle of the night and we had no idea where we were. I looked at my roommate and thought, "This was a terrible idea." From her face, I could tell she agreed.

We followed them up a flight of stairs and entered a room to find that there were two more guys. My heart dropped. I couldn't stop thinking about the fact that I was a virgin and this situation could only end with that no longer being the case. I stood there wishing I could have a do-over, but it was too late.

A moment of relief came when our escort had a short conversation and took us to another room. Why did this provide a sense of comfort? I'm not sure. I guess I was thinking our odds were better with just one stranger versus four.

We tried to make the best of the situation and began making small talk and watching a little TV. All of a sudden, someone burst through the door with a sawed-off shotgun. Yes, if you had to re-read that sentence, it was a sawed-off shotgun. As you can imagine, my roommate and I froze. I can't remember if my "date" pulled out another weapon at the time and cursed him out, but eventually it became clear they were playing. Somewhere along the way, we realized we were in the midst of a gang. Like, we were in the middle of a motel, in the middle of God knows where, with an entire gang.

Once they were finished "playing", the assailant left and we eventually began to breathe again. Sparingly, of course, but it was breathing nonetheless. My roommate and I had many silent conversations during that time. I think most of the conversation was, "Why? Why? Why?" Somehow, with my heart beating through my chest, I heard him mention needing to get his hair braided. I don't remember ever wanting to do someone's hair so badly, but it was a potential avenue to safety – killing time. If I could braid his hair, he would be occupied and we would be safe for a while.

He was so excited when I said I could braid that he immediately started collecting the tools to get his hair done. My plan was working.

Just as I began to braid, he asked my roommate to go purchase some cigarettes for him. She agreed and took his car to the store. Again, I was thinking, "Why, Lord?" I knew she had to go. I don't think either one of us wanted to upset him. I just didn't want to be alone in that situation.

I also couldn't help but worry about her driving his car. I didn't even know if she could drive. That meant we were possibly getting deeper and deeper, into an ever-evolving night of death. How could any of this end well?

I'm not exactly sure how long it took her, but I know it felt like hours. Normally, I'm a very fast braider, but this time, I couldn't seem to get it right. I knew if I finished too soon and she wasn't back, it would be over for me. So, I braided slowly, as he grew impatient. He said things like, "Where the fuck is she?" and "She's taking too damn long." I was thinking the same exact thing. When she finally came back, I was on the last braid and had never been happier to see her.

After I finished his hair, he got dressed and told us he'd be right back. We never saw him again.

An hour or so after he left, a random guy came into the room with a chick and kicked us out. He told us that my "date" wasn't coming back and we couldn't stay there. We were so happy. We grabbed our things and all but ran out the door. We had no idea where we were. It was the middle of the night, our phones were dying, and we didn't know who to call. Our relief slowly turned into a different kind of panic.

As we walked out of the motel, we found ourselves in front of a strip club on a street we'd never been on, across from a run-down apartment that apparently hosted many of Atlanta's best prostitutes. It had to be about five o'clock in the morning when we finally got picked up by my roommate's friend from back home. We were in tears when she picked us up. The whole situation was a complete mess.

For much of my college experience, God affirmed who He was in my life. That night, God became a real Protector to me. I didn't realize how God had been protecting me my whole life, until I was forced to see it in such a "real" way. That was the first time

I'd experienced God watching over me and I knew it couldn't have been anything but Him keeping me safe.

I remember telling the story to my friends and they were in total disbelief. I was chastised over and over again and it was well deserved. I was so relieved to have a relationship with God and be alive, I didn't care what people thought.

My roommate and I could have been raped or killed. Yet, we made it home, unharmed, and safe. I have to give that credit to God. Thankfully, the majority of my dating experiences weren't like that. I actually had a lot of fun dating freshman year. Maybe even too much fun.

I didn't have an interest in a relationship, as much as I enjoyed meeting new people and experiencing new things. Dating was "hanging out" with the occasional kiss or two. Something about "having options" made me feel powerful and in control. I had already experienced an amazing boyfriend; I wanted to know what else was out there.

Unfortunately, this mindset put me in a position to hurt people. I don't know what the guys wanted that I dated. I didn't really care. I just knew what I wanted and that was "a good time". It was a very emotionless approach to dating, which resurfaced in an even worse way later on in my story.

At that point in my life, I wasn't totally heartless yet. I developed feelings for a close friend by the end of the year. He was actually a preacher – the type of person I would have never imagined myself dating. It's strange how it all happened. I don't remember either one of us being strongly physically attracted to each other. I just remember feeling a strong pull to him. I'm not sure what it was but it was eventually made clear that, "Good Vibes" don't always equate to romantic chemistry.

At the end of freshman year, nearing summer break, my friend and I shared our feelings for each other. It was very indirect. I remember telling my roommate what I thought happened, but I wasn't sure. To make things even more confusing, we carried on afterwards as if we never talked about our feelings.

Over the summer, a lot changed in my life. I moved back home to work, hoping to live off campus and purchase a new car. My initial plan was to room with my freshman year roommate from San Diego, but somewhere along the way, I ended up living back home permanently and commuting.

After the summer break, my freshman year relationships were either strengthened or they completely vanished. Neither of my freshman year roommates returned for sophomore year and I didn't have many friends from Spelman.

This left me with my Morehouse brothers, grouped into two separate families. There were "The Preachers" and "The Bio Boys." As if it needs further explanation, one group was filled with philosophy and religion majors who were all preachers or ministers. The other group was also Christian men, but they were pre-med majors. The only girl that was consistently around sophomore year was Za. Freshman year, we seemed to be in different places, but by sophomore year, we were back to our old selves again.

That year was like my "high on Jesus" incubation period. If Desmond helped me with my spiritual foundation, this year was like higher learning. Sometimes I look back to that time, wondering if I will ever get that close to God again. In my heart, I feel that God is always near. It's just my awareness that has to change. At that point in my life, I knew

God was walking beside me and I never doubted it. I lived it and I lived differently knowing it.

In those moments, I was in a place where I had little distractions and everyone around me wanted to see God in ways they never had before. Those moments were some of the weirdest and best moments in my life. I learned so much about what it meant to have a relationship with God that I believe it will carry me for the rest of my life.

I remember praying and fasting and seeing changes in my life, my family, and my friends. I remember talking to God on a daily basis and witnessing miracles again and again. I also remember experiencing some of the "dangers" of growing close to God written somewhere in the depths of our sinful nature.

To expound, let's consider Adam and Eve. They had everything they needed, could walk and talk with God freely and they still weren't satisfied. Something about being close to God brings out one of the most difficult kinds of temptation. Especially when you start smelling yourself.

It's easy to reach a certain place with God and feel entitled, or misinterpret God's Word because you begin to stop seeking to understanding with humility. I remember walking around feeling like I knew the secrets to the universe and no one else knew. In essence, that's not bad. It's looking at people differently or valuing yourself differently because of your experiences that can destroy you. There's also this idea that you know all there is to know. As if God can't teach you anything else. That can be dangerous. These thoughts were building in me as I grew in Christ. It wasn't long before it would jump up and bite me in the butt.

The benefits of my walk outweighed my own self-righteous struggles. Again, I've never felt closer to

God than in those times. I had also never personally experienced God as a Healer, a Friend, and so many other things. My preacher friends created a safe place for me to learn what it really meant to be in relationship with God. Since there were so many things that happened during that time, I'll just give a couple examples.

I was actually dating the friend that I mentioned previously – the one that I had that conversation about our feelings with. We finally talked and decided that dating was an option. It was a weird experience because I don't know if either one of us had an expectation that it would be a long-term thing. It was just like, "I like you. You like me. Let's try this out."

So, we were on the phone, talking about some of the challenges I had with the gift of tongues. I was explaining how I grew up in a Pentecostal church and although it wasn't deliberately stated, basically, you weren't saved if you didn't speak in tongues. After studying, praying, and growing in my relationship with God, I knew that wasn't true. I explained to him that I rejected the idea of speaking in tongues because I didn't agree with how it was presented to me.

After delivering my argument, my boyfriend told me that God wanted to give me the gift of tongues if it was something I wanted. He also shared that if it was something I wanted, it would happen when the group of preachers and I were back together again

I remember feeling conflicted. One part of me was extremely curious because it was something I always wondered about. The other part of me was scared. I didn't know what that experience would be like.

Regardless, the conversation ended and so did my thoughts about speaking in tongues. The day my preacher friends and I were reunited was relatively normal. We caught up, joked, laughed, and did what we always do. Eventually, I remember all of us delving into a deep conversation, and helping one of our friends work through some sort of a mental dilemma.

After hours and hours of talking, I was tired. The situation seemed to be resolved and I was getting ready to head out the door. At that point, one of the guys stated that they needed to pray for me. I thought it was weird, so I begrudgingly replied, "Ok, sure."

As they prayed, I remember one of them asking if I wanted to receive the gift of speaking in tongues. I said, "Yes," and somewhere in the midst of the prayer I became overwhelmed. In the midst of my praise, my words changed and my knees became weak.

It's difficult to explain exactly what happened, but the end result was me speaking in a strange language I'd never spoken before. Initially, it sounded a lot like babble, but quickly grew into sounds that sounded more like words or phrases. In addition to this new "tongue," spiritually, I was on fire. I could hear God giving me scriptures for friends and words to speak into their lives. God was even responding to my needs before I even got a chance to ask.

One day, I received a scripture for Za and God used her to bless me in a way that still amazes me today. The semester just began and I had absolutely no books. I didn't usually read the books I was assigned, so I wasn't terribly worried, but I do remember the need to purchase them crossing my mind. One night, I had a strange dream where I received a check for four hundred dollars. In my dream, my first thought was, "Now I can purchase my books for school."

When I woke up, I thought it was the weirdest thing. I'd never dreamt about getting money before. I'd also never had a dream that was more than just a dream either. I kind of shrugged it off and proceeded to go about my day as normal.

Later at the coffee shop on campus, I was studying and received a call from Za. Somewhere in the conversation, Za asked me if I had gotten my books for school yet. I laughed and told her I wasn't worried about it, but I wasn't planning on getting them because I didn't have the money.

She went on to share that it was funny I said that because when she woke up, she had a strong pull on her heart concerning me. She said she had a feeling that she needed to give me half of her savings to go towards my books. Immediately, my heart stopped and I felt myself pushing my phone deeper into the side of my face. I asked her how much was in her savings and she responded, "$800."

I can't even begin to explain my feelings when she said that. All I could do was shake my head as tears streamed down my face. I told her about my dream and she immediately went to the bank and brought me the money in cash.

It was probably one of the first times I'd ever seen something supernatural develop into something tangible. It changed my life. Later that year, we spent our spring break on a road trip to Texas to visit a few churches, including Joel Olsten's and T.D. Jakes'. All-in-all, it was a pretty amazing year for Jesus and I.

Over the summer, I secured a job working at a Christian camp for inner-city children in Cleveland,

GA. I learned about the job from a guy I casually dated my freshman year of college, which takes me back to the dangers of emotionless dating. Even though that was probably the pinnacle of my "Good Girl" status, there was some backlash from my explorative days in college. This guy wasn't someone I considered as anything more than a friend. He was a very nice guy that I met during an open mic night at our on-campus coffee shop. One of us was leaving and we shared a few words. I'm pretty sure I said something remotely flirtatious and he responded.

We spent a lot of time together, talking, going to movies, and plays, but in my mind, it was innocent. What made it complicated was, one – we did share a few kisses, and two – he developed feelings that I couldn't reciprocate. He'd asked me several times about a relationship and although I said I would pray about it, it wasn't going to happen.

During the summer break of freshman year, he went off to this camp and met a girl. I was so happy for him. I thought he was genuinely a nice guy and I wanted him to be happy. When we saw each other again, we hung out and talked and I thought everything was fine. He was dating and so was I. Again, in my mind, it was innocent. My boyfriend didn't seem to mind our friendship at all. He was pretty laid back and he had a lot of friendships with other women, so he couldn't say too much. The guy's girlfriend, on the other hand, did not share the same sentiments.

I remember him telling me that she had some issues with our relationship because of a late night phone call, which in her defense, was pretty late. Yet, it was my first time hearing of her having an issue with me. He told me she didn't want him to be on the phone with me after a certain time and that was that in my mind.

To be absolutely honest, I thought it was ridiculous for several reasons. One, I felt like we never had a deep romance, so we were really just friends. Two, both of us were in relationships. Lastly, if he was on the phone until "too late" that was on him, not me. In retrospect, my perspective was very insensitive, but those were my young, raw emotions.

With all of that, camp was really awkward. I was able to meet his girlfriend prior to camp, but by that point she already hated me. Later, she told me I should have made an effort to meet her long before camp. I tried to be understanding and sensitive to her feelings, but I truthfully did not understand.

I also began to have negative feelings towards him. I felt like he wasn't in control of the situation and it was causing me to have to deal with something that should have been handled in-house. I remember camp becoming extremely stressful with all of my failed attempts at avoiding that situation. So much so, it consumed my prayer life and I found myself dreaming about her. I do believe my dreams were helpful hints on how to address her, which was what I was praying for.

One night, I had a nightmare about her that caused me to avoid her the next day. Interestingly enough, she seemed to be avoiding me as well. The next night, I had a dream she was happy and welcoming and that day her family was there. She was so happy, she not only spoke to me that day, but she personally introduced me to her family.

That summer pretty much solidified my "Church Girl" status. I could spend the rest of this book discussing my many amazing spiritual encounters, but that's not what this book is about. This book is about how I lost myself.

THE LOST CHILD

"Losing oneself is like falling. It's a gradual process."

It's difficult to pinpoint exactly when I began to fall, which isn't too different from a physical fall. You don't remember the moment you began to fall, as much as you remember the moment you realized you were falling. Falling was a very long, mental process for me. Much like establishing my identity – but things always seem to take less time being torn apart than being built up.

My story is much like that. It took about two years to break what was built in twenty-one. The first question, amongst a host of others to come that began to deconstruct my very being, crept in my junior year of college. It was so simple, yet so devastating. "Why do I have to be so different?"

In retrospect, the thought was filled with arrogance. I genuinely felt like I had to be better than everyone else. When dealing with Christian women, I felt I had to be more caring and sensitive to their emotions, when in reality I didn't care about all of their unaddressed insecurities, nor did I feel like offering pleasantries I didn't feel I was afforded. I didn't care that a lot of Christian women seemed to be attracted to Christianity because they felt "less than." As if insecurity was a qualifier for loving Christ. Of course, there's room for everyone in God, but there was a trend of the Christian women I met lacking confidence in who they were and hiding away in the rituals of religion.

It was such a false sense of humility. I didn't care that they couldn't stand to be around beautiful women. I didn't care that they seemed to have a strange obsession with "protecting" their relationships, when in fact, no one wanted their men in the first place. That was, in all honesty, their problem.

The other side of that was no better. There was the Christian woman who was so confident, she literally held her nose up to look down at everyone else.

Almost as if she was too holy to acknowledge anyone else as a human being. These women were relatively unapproachable, but usually held some position in the church, validating that they were obviously more important.

It was difficult finding Christian women who were both down-to-earth and confident. Those women who knew they were beautiful and enjoyed appreciating the beauty in others. I can count the times I met those women and when I did, I made a point to push my need for a new friend on them. I thank God, to this day, for those relationships.

I wasn't building relationships with non-Christians. I was in constant inner-conflict with how to be a Christian – as I knew to be – and interact with others who didn't believe what I believed. I didn't want to be too spiritual and turn people off. Yet, I didn't want to be too worldly and give the wrong impression.

Ironically, being the light of the world with no one to shed light on is pretty ineffective, to say the least.

In my family, I was trying to keep up a false sense of perfection. On one side, I liked the praise and on the other, I knew all of my imperfections. I was ashamed of all of my "dirty little secrets." Maybe they weren't "as bad" as someone else's, but I felt guilty about my flaws. My Christian views were still based on me being perfect, and I knew that even if everyone else thought I was perfect, I wasn't. I was also no longer okay with that being the case.

Even with my friends, I dealt with an inner conflict. I knew they loved and accepted me, but I was still the naive and "inexperienced" one. I couldn't be a part of every conversation. I felt left out and I think they struggled with helping me to feel included because they didn't really understand what it was like for me.

It was also becoming glaringly obvious that not all Christians were walking their faith out the same way I was. I'm not sure this should have bothered me as much as it did, but it did. It seemed like everyone was living a different life and I was running a race against myself. I was depriving myself of "normal" human desires, which basically summarizes my mental state during my junior year of college. A war raged inside of me. I asked myself, "Why do you have to be better than everyone else?" "What are you trying to prove?" "If everyone else is doing what they want, then why can't you?" I had lost my ability to fight the questions with answers I actually believed.

Somewhere in that year, my mindset switched from wanting more of God to "doing good" for God. During sophomore year, I had so many amazing experiences with God, but that rollercoaster became hard to ride. It was filled with extreme highs and intense lows. I either felt like I was superhuman or failing God in some way.

In those discouraging times, I tried to maintain what I knew was right. I went back to trying to do "good works." I was trying to earn back the spiritual high. I had somehow un-learned how to function as an everyday Christian and was steadily losing interest in being the "good girl." It was too stressful and relatively unrewarding.

To add insult to injury, I was single and steadily building resentment. My boyfriend and I broke up and I distanced myself from the preachers. I had yet to experience a truly bad relationship, but neither of my relationships had worked out and I blamed my exes. (Of course, that was the only logical thing to do.)

I was still very limited in my physical experiences, but I did dabble in PG versions of lust, which brought on a lot of guilt. Although, in all of my experiences, both parties were equally responsible, I still blamed the guys. I didn't want to take personal responsibility for my own part in it, which spawned a slew of its own seeds. The question that screamed within me was, "What's the point in dating a Christian guy, if they're no different than any other guy? Aren't they all just after the same thing?"

Once these questions and feelings of isolation crept into my mind, they viciously grew in my heart. I began to measure every aspect of my life against these questions and by the end of my junior year, something in me changed. I no longer longed to be a part of the Christian lifestyle in the way that I had been before. I just wasn't ready to verbalize it.

My twenty-first birthday marked the beginning of a new era. As a "good Christian girl", I never drank alcohol. I did that because the Bible tells us to

"Obey the laws of the land." As you can imagine, once I turned twenty-one, that rule no longer applied to me because I was legal and ready to get wasted. Well, not exactly. I was legal and ready to drink, but I was committed to not be drunk. Drunkenness was still against the rules.

I had my first mixed drink at a lounge, surrounded by friends on my twenty-first birthday. To this day, I think it was the worst drink I've ever had in my life. Mostly because it was a mixed drink that was supposed to be good, but tasted like five shots of some of the strongest alcohol ever. Fortunately, or unfortunately, I didn't let that stop me from experimenting in the future.

By the time school began, I had shifted my focus from spiritual development to professional development and personal experiences. It was my senior year and every day I was inching closer and closer to the real world, which was extremely intimidating. I was determined to be successful, but I was no longer as confident in who I wanted to be as an individual.

Thankfully, I was in a very good position senior year. I lucked out with a great roommate and the perfect living space. We were the first residents of our school's newest dorm – an apartment-style dorm that was the envy of all the other dorms. We had a two-bedroom apartment with living room space, a kitchenette, and a bathroom. It was like living off campus, without having the commute.

My living space was perfect, my roommate was perfect, and I was focused. My goals were to keep my part-time job as an after-school teacher, make all A's, figure out what I wanted to do with my life, and have lots and lots of fun. Putting major emphasis on the "lots and lots" of fun. It's funny how easy it is to get lost in a place of complacency. In my situation, that place was disguised as comfort.

What more was there to want? I was completely in control.

Za and I decided to kick off Senior Year with a house party that was supposed to kick-off the start of an amazing year. Unfortunately, the party never happened. I'm not sure why we waited around. It may have had something to do with the guy we met that night or our over-commitment to making the year memorable. I wonder now, how different my life would have been if we had just left.

When we arrived at where the party was supposed to be and found no party, Za called the number on the flyer. The promoter assured her that the party was still on, but things were running late. He was also late, but was only minutes away with the DJ. When the promoter arrived, he was distraught, although he covered it up with charm and laughter. He was extremely persuasive despite the fact that it was the party bomb of the year.

As we waited, I don't remember talking to him much. He talked with Za, while Za and I kept each other entertained. As nothing developed into more nothing, we finally gave in and went to the car to leave.

That's when things got weird. Through a distraction disguised as fate. He followed us to the car and insisted I take his number. I was completely caught off guard. As I tried to review the night in my mind, I couldn't understand why he wanted me to take his number. We couldn't have exchanged more than a few words all night and I didn't even look at him for longer than a few seconds. Yet, he intently insisted that I take his number. So, I did.

Although I was reluctant, he made me promise I'd call. I felt excited. I had just made a commitment to an exciting new year and I'd met someone new. This had to be a sign of what was to come.

When school began, my main objective was to figure out "Life after college". I was a psychology major who felt completely intimidated by a PhD program, yet had no interest in entering the workforce right after school. With some guidance, I decided to look into MSW programs.

As life was seemingly coming together, I was exchanging texts with the promoter. It wasn't very long before we made arrangements for our first one-on-one hang out. Being the "down-to-earth" girl that I was, we made plans to hang out at his place and watch a movie. The perfect scenario for something more.

I have no idea what movie we watched. I just remember feeling anxious. Although, I don't remember paying him much mind when we first met, he had somehow captivated all of my curiosity at that point. He was a mystery that I wanted to figure out. His room was small, not too messy and not too neat. There was nothing that gave anything about him away.

To add to the puzzle, he avoided most questions with awkward laughter and the introduction of new subjects. You could tell that he had been playing the game for a long time. Needless to say, the movie was a distraction to avoid conversation and led to our first kiss.

Although I don't remember the kiss, per say, I remember feeling something different about this encounter. It was something new. Something exhilarating. I had somehow lost control. He caught me off guard and I couldn't predict what would happen next. As the kiss intensified, he began reaching for my zipper and I put my hand on top of his, as I snapped back to reality.

I was all too used to sharing that I was a virgin with any man who wanted to try me, but there was something about that moment that made me feel reluctant. For the first time, I felt ashamed of it. We shared a few uncomfortable laughs and after it was confirmed that it really wasn't going to happen, we parted ways. I left and all I could think about was that kiss and what if. What if I never stopped him?

When my first boyfriend and I ended things freshman year, I was very open to hangouts much like these. The only difference was that again, I had no problem letting guys know that I had no intention of going any farther than a kiss. It was something I flirted with frequently, but I never feared going too far. It wasn't something I never wanted.

At the time, I thought it was something about him. In retrospect, it wasn't him at all. I was enticed by something else. It was something that had been enticing me for quite some time. I no longer wanted to be "good."

All of my little questions from junior year eventually funneled into one big question – "Why am I still a virgin?" The epitome of my mental struggle transformed into a final act of defiance. It was a question that directly attacked my standard of morality and my response would seal my fate.

That's not to say that anyone who loses their virginity before marriage has no standard of morality. All this says is that my sole purpose in keeping my virginity was to honor God with my body. If that question was presented any earlier, it would have been shot down with precision and little to no second thought. Yet, somehow it landed perfectly in my mind's intense line of questioning and lingered.

In the previous year, I had learned that pretty much all of my Christian friends were having sex. Thinking back, I was just naïve. Maybe that's what shattered my world. I had a narrow viewpoint of what it meant to be a Christian and I was upset that God wasn't as exclusive as I believed Him to be. It wasn't so much about having done something wrong, asking for forgiveness, and moving on. I didn't understand how one could "live in sin" and still love God. Let alone, God still love you.

I was filled with pride and I couldn't see it. I remember talking to my closest friends and telling them I didn't see the point in keeping my virginity when everyone else was having sex. They were very adamant about me keeping up the good fight, but they loved it. They loved sex and they couldn't hide it.

I remember one night specifically, two of my friends told me I shouldn't start having sex because it was hard to stop. Then they would slip into a conversation about how addictive it was. I felt invisible. It wasn't their fault. They were telling the truth and that was their reality. I just didn't understand why I still had to be the sex-less one. From the outside looking in, it was like everyone was at this amazing party I wasn't invited to. Yet, they told me it wasn't really any fun to make me feel better. All of these seeds and questions, combined with lots of sexual tension between the promoter and I brought me to my knees.

That was my turning point – a night I will never forget. My roommate must have been gone because I spent a significant part of my night pleading with God. I threw all of the questions that had been plaguing me back at Heaven, angrily awaiting a response to no avail. Honestly, I was demanding a response.

"Lord, why do I have to be different? Why does it matter what I do if you love us all the same? Why God?"

Like a spoiled brat, I cried out to God about all the things I felt I was missing out on because of His rules. God responded in a quiet and gentle voice. Through my tears, I heard in the deepest parts of my heart, "You were made for this." It was like God was pleading, too. I know He had no desire for me to take the hard road. He had another way set out for me, yet that brought me no comfort. It just furthered my anguish.

"Made for what, God? Torture? Was I made to endure torture? For what?" I cried on the floor in the corner of my perfect room, during my triumphant senior year, and God continued to repeat the same thing over and over.

I want to say that I live life with no regrets, but it's difficult to say that when I can see that day so clearly in my mind. I wanted to tell myself to listen to God, but that's not how the story went. I don't remember if I said it out loud or just in my heart, but that conversation ended with an official resignation of my beliefs in living a "Christian" lifestyle. I quit. When I got up from the floor, something shifted. I was taking control of my life and it was literally the worst decision I've ever made.

Now, it wasn't a matter of "if" I was going to lose my virginity but when and to whom. The promoter and I had become closer, but in a distant acquaintance kind of way. We enjoyed great conversation, occasionally made out, but he really brought a lot of insight into the male mind.

One conversation I remember explicitly was about the type of guys who would take a woman's virginity. He told me that some guys don't sleep with virgins because of the emotional attachment, while others enjoyed the attachment. I was confused as to why a woman losing her virginity would end in an emotional trance, but I listened.

He explained that sex was physical for men, not necessarily emotional. For women, it was emotional. I knew I wasn't going to be that girl. I was determined not to be that girl. I had already packaged my heart up in a nice and tidy box somewhere deep inside of myself, so becoming emotional was not an option. He did share that he was not that type of guy that would take someone's virginity. Although, I didn't believe him I was not convinced I want him to be "that guy" anyway.

At the end of the day, I decided that I wanted what I wanted. I could say that I didn't deliberately shut off God's voice, but I would be lying. I chose not to hear what He had to say. I chose not to care how He felt. I wasn't interested in love. At that point, I felt I had experienced love. I wasn't under the impression that sex equated to love. I just wanted to know what all the fuss was all about. Again, I had no intention of being "that girl".

The promoter and I had already come close so many times, that I made it up in my mind that it could not be him. At that point, we were on our way to being friends and I didn't want it to be awkward. In addition, I was afraid he was the only person that could possibly throw a wrench in my plans of sex with no emotional attachment. The scenario was so much more logical for me.

He was a player. I knew that from day one and it wasn't something he tried to hide. Nor was it something that mattered to me for who we were to each other. I just didn't want to get hurt. I came to the conclusion that although I wanted to be with him in that way, sleeping with someone who I had no feelings for would be so much easier. In theory, I wouldn't have to be worried about being emotionally attached because there were no feelings to begin with.

Even in entertaining these thoughts, I was drifting worlds away from who I once was. I wrestled with it for months. The thing that was missing from my emotionless scenario was a possible alternative specimen.

One day, I was hanging out at the college café, minding my own business, when a familiar face stopped by. It was an acquaintance from freshman year. That acquaintance also happened to be a very tall, dark, and very handsome, young man. At that point, we had this never-ending, flirt-in-passing thing going on. It was fun, but I had no intention of taking it further. I guess I wasn't sure how much of it was a game and how much of it was real.

As always, when he saw me, he smiled and pulled me in for a hug. Surprisingly, this time he sat down with me and started a conversation, which was something new for us. He asked what I was doing, and I shared that I was looking up recipes to bake a pie from scratch. Unknowingly, I had just opened the door I had been looking for.

His face lit up instantaneously. He revved about his love of cooking and invited me to come over to make the pie together. He also made sure to express his continued interest in me over the years. For the first time, I genuinely considered his flirtation as the potential for something more. We exchanged information and planned a baking date.

Within a week or so, I was on the way to the chef's house while on the phone with Za trying to work through my growing dilemma with the promoter. I remember telling her that we seemed to be getting closer and closer to having sex, but I didn't feel like that was the best thing for me.

After getting off the phone with Za, I walked into the chef's house, completely unassuming. My mind was everywhere, which may have been why I gravely underestimated the get-together. I saw it like many of my other hang-outs – the opportunity to get to know him better. Yet, nothing had been the same since that moment in the room with God.

He opened the door with a smile and was a complete gentleman. He introduced me to his roommate and we immediately got to baking. It was fun. We worked through the entire process together in between laughs and wine. I documented the entire event with pictures and we put the pie in the oven to bake.

He then took the fruit peels and began sautéing them with sugar. It was pretty fun to watch him do his thing. He was a cool guy and our time was rather therapeutic, especially with the head space I was in. While we waited for the pie to finish baking, we went to watch a movie in his bedroom. I had seen the movie before, so it ended up being background noise as we talked. We lay on his bed, side-by-side, in a very platonic manner. My guard was completely down.

Maybe twenty minutes into the movie, he asked if he could give me a massage. I agreed. I love massages. So I lay flat on my stomach. He asked to unbutton my bra. I agreed and he began his massage. It was great. So great, I began to drift off to sleep.

With my eyes closed, somewhere in the middle of consciousness and unconsciousness, I felt a soft kiss on my lower back. It literally sent chills up and down my spine. Needless to say, that night took a turn down a completely different road from baking pie.

Somewhere in our time together, I shared that I was a virgin and had no intention of having sex and again, he was the perfect gentleman. I mean, at least for where we were. He shared that he understood and didn't want to pressure me. Yet, for whatever reason, that made him even more desirable. That night, I lost my virginity.

Well, I actually gave it away, willingly. He was patient, kind, gentle, and considerate. He even asked me to stay with him the morning after, but I couldn't. Right after it was over, my emotional subconscious checked back in. I needed to figure out how I felt, which meant I needed to get as far away from him as possible.

I remember calling Za and my cousin, Charlotte, on my way to my mother's house. I don't remember if they answered or what they said. I just remember tears slowly streaming down my face. It was like my heart knew how I felt before I did. My brain was still processing.

When I finally realized what I had done, something broke inside of me. After all of my internal turmoil, all of my pleading, and questioning, I felt nothing. Even in light of a relatively "great" first time, sex brought me nothing I thought I'd gain. Sex was sex, an experience that I could have lived without for just a while longer and I officially lost what was "unique" about me.

I was no longer the good girl. I was no longer the virgin. I was no longer really living the "Christian" life, according to my own standards. I was just like everybody else. Now we were all in the same race and I hated that feeling.

I thought back on a pact I made with a friend before she lost her virginity. We shared our struggles and decided that in order to hold each other accountable, whoever lost their virginity first was responsible for the other. She lost her virginity a few months prior to me and I still couldn't hold her responsible for what I had done. In all my logic concerning how I would feel about who I slept with,

I never factored in how sleeping with someone would make me feel about myself.

Losing my virginity the way I did, made me feel more alone. Now, I fit in with the group I wasn't really sure I wanted to.

So I grew a shell. In order to not hate myself, I had to stop caring about who I was and embrace who I had become. I decided that no one needed to know who I really was. All they needed to see was that I was strong, smart, and successful. And somewhere in my shell, I became delusional. I decided I was proud of the new me.

I don't remember talking to the chef much after our initial encounter, nor did I have any feelings about it. Not only was I officially a woman, but I was a woman who was successfully emotionally unattached to sex.

Sex became an even deeper obsession. Not necessarily in practice, but in the way that it overran my thoughts. I had so many questions and so many people to learn from. It was an adrenaline rush, just thinking about the possibilities of my new experience.

My promoter friend seemed to have mixed feelings about my first encounter and lots of questions. He wanted a play-by-play of everything that happened and I was eagerly candid with information. I'm not sure how much he appreciated that, but I went on, knowing he of all people couldn't complain. We were in a weird place, somewhere between lovers and friends. I felt like having sex with someone else gave me power in my relationship with the promoter. I refused to willingly give him power over me. He thought I was crazy and I may have been but I specifically told him that I didn't want to fall for him.

Life was peaceful for a while. I enjoyed my winter break, took some time to myself, and resumed school in January. Time was furiously ticking towards "the end" of my childhood. School was almost over and I had a lot of decisions to make. School continued to be relatively easy, but I grew anxious awaiting the decisions from the graduate programs I'd applied to. I attended a few job fairs and thought of how unprepared I was for the real world. I was praying that I would get accepted somewhere.

Romantically, things were quiet for a month or two. The promoter was still around in the same capacity and I wasn't dating. I also wasn't having sex. I had no intention of having sex with any and every one. I had the experience and that was satisfying for a time. At least for a time.

Unfortunately, opening Pandora's Box is very difficult to close. One night I got the text from the promoter that forever changed our relationship. It went something like, "I'm headed home. Come over." It was late, so there were only so many options for entertainment. I responded back quickly with, "okay." We spent the night together and at the time, it was great. It was exactly what I wanted. I knew he was with other women, so I had no expectations on the longevity of a romance. I just wanted to feed my flesh. So that's what I did.

Sometime in early spring, I received my acceptance to GA State University's MSW program. Overjoyed was an understatement. If there was anything I knew how to do, it was school, and that was with little to no effort. My next two years were secure and I could finally solely focus on having fun. Spring Break was quickly approaching and my friends and I were planning a trip to Miami, so I offered the promoter a ride with us.

Prior to leaving for Miami, I met another self-entitled "good guy," and although I'd recently sworn them off, I decided to give him a chance. Za and I actually met him at a restaurant where he was our server. He was Christian and was very adamant about taking me on a date, so I obliged. We went on a date and talked on the phone, but I had a hard time trusting him. All I could think of was, "'good guys' don't exist."

One day, he came by Spelman and we sat in his car and talked for a while. Somehow the conversation landed on the topic of sex. I reluctantly shared that I recently lost my virginity. He kept repeating, "really," in a state of disbelief.

While you may be thinking he was judging me, he seemed to be doing quite the opposite. After he finally took my "yes" as confirmation that I did, in fact, lose my virginity, he began expressing how hard abstinence was. Although it seemed very suggestive in the wrong kind of way. To me, that was all the confirmation I needed to solidify "good guys" were in fact, a myth.

It was like he was saying he was abstinent with his mouth and expressing he would like to "tear it down" via telepathic energy waves. I couldn't see how us talking about how badly we wanted to have sex was going to help us abstain from anything. Besides, I wasn't abstinent. I was having sex. Just not with him.

Maybe it was where I was mentally and emotionally, or maybe he felt we were closer than we were. Regardless, it was a major turn off. He could have been completely innocent, but it just seemed like a ploy to get somewhere he wasn't going to get.

In addition, he followed that conversation with asking me to send him pictures while I was in Miami. I responded by asking if he wanted pictures of the beach. Of course, he wanted pictures of me on the beach. I didn't understand how my half-naked pictures would help him in his struggle. Again, it was confirmation that men were men. Period.

Needless to say, we didn't keep in touch, but my friends and I had an unforgettable time on our three-day trip to Miami. The trip was epic indeed. So epic that we all agreed Miami would only be kept in our minds and not in any other form of incriminating evidence. Therefore, I can only say that it set the tone for my future party life. I experienced my first shots, extreme drunkenness – among other things – and a permanent reminder of "Spring Break '09."

Spring break was a glimpse into my dark future that was quickly approaching. At the time, it felt like the first time I truly let myself go. I was finally gaining the control I so desperately wanted.

With all of my new bad habits, I was also helping the promoter get his marketing and promotion business off the ground. Although, he was doing parties at the time, he wanted to do something bigger, which I wanted to help him with. I admire anyone who has the guts to pursue their dreams. I admire, even more so, people who can make their dreams come true.

At the time, I viewed him as a twenty-one year-old who had some hardships and was trying to build something. So, I helped him as much as I could.

In the midst of all of this, God was still trying to reach me. But, I was too far gone. One night, I remember having a strange dream about the promoter. We were riding in a car that seemed to be breaking down. Somewhere in the middle of our trip, he got out of the car and went a different way.

I think it was hard to understand what it meant at the time, because it wasn't what I wanted our relationship to be. Yet, it was. The dream predicted a ride that was going nowhere. At the time, I reconciled it as confirming that he was lost, but I would help find him. I can imagine God sitting in heaven sending every sign he could possibly throw to say, "Wrong Way!" "Danger!" as I jogged with my eyes closed, hoping not to trip and fall. Even then, He was with me.

Outside of spiritual signs, there were some very practical red flags that I completely ignored. One of those red flags popped up during a trip to Wal-mart, when I went with him to pick up his contact lenses. While I was sitting next to him, the woman at the front desk asked him for his information, which was normal.

She then asked, "What's your date of birth?" He followed with the month, date, and year. Which would have also been normal, if the year hadn't completely shifted my understanding of how old he was.

I remember that moment so clearly in my mind. It was one of the weirdest things I had ever experienced. There I was, sitting at a doctor's office with someone who I thought I had a pretty good idea about, in a general sense, and I had no idea who he was.

I thought, "What did he say?" and again, as if God was dropping hints, the woman asked him to repeat it. I kept my head down, this time listening ten times more intently. He repeated the same month, and the same day, and the same year which was a whole three years older than I thought he was. I could not wipe the shock from my face.

I remember texting Za while we were still at Walmart to ask what age you had to be if you were born in that year. After she responded, I told her what happened and she, too, was shocked. Neither of us really knew what that meant. Somehow we settled on the idea that he had a fake ID because he wouldn't lie about his age, right?

I couldn't fathom why someone would lie about their age. I was used to the idea that people pretended to be older, but younger? I didn't get it. So, as time went on, I suppressed the thought. I guess I couldn't imagine that he would lie to me like that.

An even bigger red flag happened the week before I graduated. While trying to prepare for finals, I got a call from a mutual friend who dropped a major bomb. The promoter had been arrested. And to add to the shock, she needed me to meet her to get his keys. I must give a disclaimer; although he lied, he didn't come off as a major lawbreaker. He just wasn't that type of guy. Yet, here I was, picking up the keys of a guy I barely knew to watch his place and dog for some undisclosed amount of time.

Somehow this very carefree fling was evolving into something else entirely. I was deeply conflicted. I didn't want to leave him hanging, but I was preparing for my last week in college. With all of the girls in his life, it seemed like at least one of them would have been more available for this job.

The entire ordeal was probably two or three days, but it seemed like forever. There was very little information given and although I did get some help, it wasn't enough to make it not seem like such a burden. I can't describe the joy I felt hearing his voice at the end of the third day, when he asked me to pick him up from the train station.

Once he came back, it was like nothing happened. I was a little more inquisitive, but I was comfortable where we were. He was in his space, I was in mine, and we met in the middle.

School ended, the summer came, and his life became increasingly more turbulent, as I became increasingly more involved. It really could have been that his life was always that way, he was just sharing a lot more. Either way, he had a way of pulling me in. He was in and out of places to stay and had an unreliable car, but the more time we spent together, the more time I wanted to spend with him.

By the time grad school began, we were sharing a room rental in the city. I wanted him to be stable. I thought if I could help him settle down, it would be better for the both of us. I also thought it would be cool to have a place to stay in the city to be closer to school. The plan was simple. We were friends with benefits helping each other out. Not complicated at all.

It didn't take long for our relationship to take the plunge. The one where you know you're falling, but there's no longer anything to hold on to. I told him I was preparing to go on a date with a friend of a friend from Morehouse, which was not uncommon. We talked about relationships with other people all the time. Yet, now that I think about it, we only talked about his relationships, not mine.

In telling him, my assumption was that he was going to deal with it like I did. There were no feelings and we would keep it that way. Instead, he responded by saying, "Don't go out with him," with his, "I'm just kidding, but not really" smile. I remember looking at him and saying, "Why not? We're not exclusive." He said, "Well, let's be exclusive then."

I didn't trust him. Well, maybe that's not true. I did trust him to be true to who he'd shown me he was. I trusted him to sleep with girls, throw parties, and tell me what he wanted to tell me. That's what I knew. That's what I had grown accustomed to. I wanted him to stay within those predictable borders. That was the only way I could keep from getting hurt. Now, he was proposing something that sounded too good to be possible. It was something I had never considered up until that point. It was the possibility of something more.

I don't remember whether I shared my thoughts with him or just agreed to try, but we did leave that conversation "exclusive." My only stipulation was that if for any reason, he couldn't do it, he would let me know immediately. He agreed. Even after having that conversation, I still went on the date. A large part of me was curious about the guy and the other part of me didn't want to play the fool. It wasn't a terrible date, but it wasn't enough to pull me back, as I had already begun leaping for the hope of what could be.

As much as the uncertainty around my newfound relationship status annoyed me, I was in it. I was living with him, and as far as I knew, he was abiding by our agreement. Even if I couldn't convince myself that he was. I think I was just scared of what a lie would do to me. At that point, I had never been lied to by a guy. Not about being with only me. Something like that could break a woman. Fortunately, the truth didn't take long to reveal itself.

One night, while asleep in our room, I had one of the shortest, most vivid dreams I can remember. Somehow, I discovered that he had kissed a girl. I woke up abruptly – enraged. All while he was sound asleep.

The dream was so life-like, it was hard to separate it from reality. I couldn't shake the feeling that he'd already betrayed me. As my heart pounded through my chest, I looked over at his phone. It didn't take much debate before I was rummaging through his text messages. I needed badly to confirm that I was overreacting and my dream was just a dream. Honestly, who would expect to find something in a guy's phone, just because they had a dream?

I surely didn't.

When I looked through the phone, it didn't take long for me to discover a kiss he shared with a girl the night before. I was devastated. Thinking back to that moment, a kiss was nothing. It was only the beginning and I should have known then that it wasn't a relationship I could emotionally invest in. I wanted so badly to go back to where we were before I was forced to trust him to be more than what I thought he could be. At that point, everything was ruined.

As I write this, Beyoncé's song, "Resentment" plays softly in my memories. "Because you lied," was all I thought about for months. He told me it was unrealistic to think he could just "quit cold-turkey." It was never my idea for him to quit in the first place. Now, I had to deal with the aftermath.

For the first time in my life, I had been cheated on. It was always one of my biggest fears, which was partly why relationships were so hard for me to get into. I had trusted someone to be committed to me and they couldn't. Now, what was I to do? I had to deal with it. I think I stayed because I knew before it happened that it wasn't going to work. I felt like I put myself in that position, so somehow I deserved the punishment. I didn't consider the option that it was okay to walk away. It was okay to be selfish with my heart.

Somewhere along the way, I was destroyed. I always knew I would never tolerate that kind of behavior, so I obviously couldn't stay. It had to be someone else. Someone who didn't realize what she was worth. Ultimately, it wasn't the action that destroyed me. It was my decision to stay.

In order to stay, I had to relinquish my self-respect. I had to relinquish my self-worth. How could I continue to identify with who I was and also be the girl who stayed with the "No-Good Guy" who couldn't commit? I couldn't. I had to be someone else.

Up until that point, I was never the insecure girl. I never claimed to be the most beautiful girl in the world, but I had no issue with that. There are plenty of girls who aren't that. I just knew that I liked me and I could live with that. Yet, this one decision was now causing all of that to crumble before my very own eyes.

It didn't take me very long to forgive him, but in doing so, I committed to facing one of my biggest fears daily. At any moment we were apart, he could be with someone else and I would never know. I would be driven into a frenzy every time it took him "too much" time to respond to a text or every time he got a call on the phone. I was literally driving myself insane.

Somewhere between August and December of that year, I died. I didn't realize I had been on life support from the moment I left God in that corner. I was just barely making it. And after that, I was a certified zombie. Dead, doped up on sex, alcohol, and parties. I finally had everything I thought I was missing and I didn't have myself. In hindsight, I can see that every inch I stepped away from who I always knew I was, I gave pieces of myself away. Sure, people change. Honestly, they should change, but not to the point where they have lost all sense of self. There's no benefit in that.

I wasn't perfect. Up until I lost my virginity, I was judgmental, narrow-minded, and prideful, but there was a lot of good in me, too. Now, all of that had gone away. I couldn't respect myself anymore. It got to a point where I hated any girl with a pretty face. Which then evolved into a hatred for anyone with a vagina because at times, it seemed like he had no preference.

I felt "less-than."

It was hard dealing with it on my own, but it was even harder trying to convince my friends that I was okay. They would ask me how I was doing and I eventually lost the ability to deceive them. It was exhausting.

They waited, hoping they could rescue me, but I wouldn't let them. I continually convinced them that I was in no need of a hero. "I'm fine, seriously." They surrendered unwillingly. I know they asked themselves if they were doing enough and they were. There was just nothing they could have done to make me think I was in need of saving.

I couldn't face myself. How could I tell them who I had become? I wanted to fade into the background, wishing desperately they would let me go.

I was so lost, depressed, and trying desperately to make our relationship mean something more than a silly girl falling for the wrong guy. I struggled between convincing my heart I could trust him and being a "good friend." It was almost like trying to retrain my brain that red was no longer red, while balancing a book on my head and riding a bike. That wasn't possible for me. Instead, I kept saying "green," seeing red, and trying to drink the truth away.

My ever-growing feelings of obligation towards him were such a huge weight on my shoulders. Within a year of meeting, he had been in at least four different unstable living situations. He seemed to lose everything he cared about. His car was unreliable. Friends were in and out of his life. I genuinely felt for him.

I don't know if it makes it better or worse that my feelings of obligation were 99.8% self-imposed. I really just wanted to be a good friend to him, but it wasn't something he ever asked of me. I was determined that if I did nothing else, I would be that. I wanted to prove to him that he could succeed in life. Redemption does exist.

By the beginning of the next year, we were living in an apartment in College Park and we were not in the best place. I still didn't trust him and I'm not sure he cared to convince me anymore. We were stuck in a place where I was still in a committed relationship that he moved in and out of.

My main focus was to get through my second semester of grad school and not do anything else to further damage my life. First semester was so difficult with everything I was dealing with in my personal life. I felt like I was failing at everything.

I was battling depression, could barely make it to class, and had an internship over an hour away, which caused physical and financial strain. Needless to say, it wasn't my best term of academic performance.

So much so, my professors didn't see much hope in me either. I remember one of my professors suggesting I go part-time after I broke down in her office crying. All I wanted to do was get some extra time to finish my assignments and she seemed to suggest that I should just give up. I was pissed. I couldn't. As much as I had lost of myself, I couldn't lose school, too.

I decided I'd rather fail then quit. I left her office praying that if God would only let me get through second semester, I would finish my degree on time.

Socially, I grew more and more numb each day. Most of the friends I made around this time had no idea who I really was. They thought I was fun, carefree, and happy. Yet, I was none of those things. My reality was much bleaker than that, but I had gotten so good at pretending, I couldn't stop.

In the midst of trying to keep what little bit of my pride I had left, I wrote the promoter an email. Hoping to come to some sort of resolution, I put all of my insecurities on the line. I told him how broken I was and how I was sure he still wasn't faithful and how I needed to know the truth. He responded by confirming all of my fears once again. He didn't affirm me, but he did give me what I asked for – the truth.

The truth hurt and I realized that wasn't what I really wanted. I wanted a fantasy where he overcame all of his issues, fell in love with me, and stopped messing with other girls. I'm not sure that I was ever in love with him. I just know I was completely consumed with him. I was devoted to him. He was the only person I was intimate with. We shared my car, took trips, shared money, met each other's families and lived together. He was a big part of my world.

Ultimately, I decided that I'd lost control and that's what I needed to get back. I couldn't convince myself to leave him. I couldn't convince myself that I didn't know what I was getting into from the beginning. I couldn't convince myself that I couldn't survive this. I just needed to adjust my thinking and take control.

I think that's the hardest part of my story to confess. In my rational mind, I can resolve everything up to that point. What's difficult to resolve is what comes from trying to assume control of things that can't be controlled. What comes from losing oneself and what can come from brokenness?

To be blunt, I'm still ashamed of what I've done. I can justify being tired, having blind faithfulness or feeling committed to someone who was not committed to me. I just can't justify my sorry attempt at revenge. I can't justify giving pieces of myself away to find wholeness in the middle of extreme brokenness, but that's exactly what I did.

In order to find solace, I did the unthinkable. I returned the favor. I sacrificed my last bit of character and thought that if I only slept with someone else, I could numb the pain. I would no longer feel worthless when he deliberately lied to me, or when he chose someone else over me. We would finally be even and I could be free again.

I remember the first time I finally embraced this idea and accepted who I had become – a shell of a woman.

That night, the promoter decided to go to a party. I wasn't interested, so I decided to hang out with an old flame. After spending some time together, I felt something close to myself again. It was freeing. The night progressed and we watched a movie. It got late, so I decided to sleep over. At some point, lying there, I thought, "this is it". So, I started to kiss him. After enough suggestion, we slept together.

The actual "act" was quite awkward, to be brutally honest. Yet, after I left, I somehow traded in my soul for a sad sense of power. I was no longer the insecure girl. The promoter was no longer in charge of my emotional well-being. I was strong again. I was not only desirable, but I could play his game just as well as he could. I could come home late. I could be with who I wanted, when I wanted and he would never know the difference. He wasn't checking for me and I wasn't checking for him.

I was naïve. Although this was a short period in my life, it was the darkest and most detrimental. If there was anything I could take back, it would have been the moments I thought giving more of myself away to someone else who meant nothing, somehow resolved the conflict in my heart.

At the time, I was creating an escape from my situation. Sex became a drug. Only to deal with the sex, I had to create and escape for that, which was drinking. Like, really drinking. To the point where any time I felt anything, I just drank until I didn't.

I remember sitting in Miami with one of my cousins and looking up how many shots it would take to die. It was me and the promoter's second trip to Miami and he invited this young girl that I knew he was messing around with. Even if he wasn't at the time, I knew he had been or would be.

Although we argued about it, nothing changed. She was still there. He was still who he was and I felt so powerless. I just wanted to feel nothing and being numb wasn't enough. I wanted to play with fate. I wanted to get as close to death as I possibly could without being responsible for it. How sad is that?

I believe my research stated that for my weight, it would take about fifteen shots to get enough alcohol in my system to die. I made it to about eight or nine shots before literally passing out. I remember crying to my cousin, while lying with my face in the toilet, telling her about how depressed I was. He was upstairs the whole time.

It was such a low moment in my life. It's still hard to give a reason as to why I let myself get there. Yet, that's the honest truth – I let myself get there. It would be so easy to blame him for "ruining my life," but he didn't. I "ruined" my life. I made the decisions that got me to where I was. I chose him.

For about five months, I led men on, used them, and lost all respect for myself. I even dated a really nice guy for a while, but I physically and emotionally wouldn't let him near me. I couldn't let him be poisoned by me. He thought I was crazy. I couldn't convince him I was dead inside and I could never be free because I didn't want to let go of the things that were killing me.

By this point, the promoter and I were completely at odds. I think as I emotionally withdrew, he grew frustrated, and we began fighting each other. Like literally blow for blow. I was in a hell I built for myself. Sometimes he would get upset and take my car for hours, while I was stuck at home. He would scream and call me names. It was a mess.

I just knew none of this was happening to me. Not me. It had to be some other crazy girl who had "Daddy issues" and never loved herself. Not me.

One day, a neighbor came to the door and told him that if he called me a bitch one more time, she would beat the shit out of him. Thankfully, the summer came and I passed all of my classes. That had to be nothing but the grace of God or really sympathetic teachers.

After first semester was over, one of my friends from the Christian camp I worked for asked me if I would return to camp as a counselor. I originally thought he was joking. It seemed both he and I were worlds away from who we use to be, but apparently he wasn't. He was going back and he wanted me to come so he would have someone there he knew.

At first, I thought it was the craziest idea ever. I was such a mess and had no business being at a camp to minister to children. Unfortunately, my home life was getting progressively worse. We were attempting to live two separate lives under the same roof with one car. The house was filled with tension and I needed space.

Going back to camp, I could no longer ignore all of the major issues I had been bandaging up for nearly two years. I was finally alone with my thoughts. Camp was about two hours from the city, in the middle of nowhere. It was creepy quiet and it was my saving grace.

I felt so out of place. Everyone knew the girl I used to be. It was like an out of body experience. I didn't even know who I'd become, so I just tried to keep my distance, but I was free. I didn't have to fight anyone for my car. I didn't have to worry about food or money. I didn't have to worry about where he was or who he was with. I was completely free.

My friend who invited me didn't even talk to me while we were at camp. God seemed to have other plans. He finally had me alone to Himself. It was perfect. That summer, I was reminded of what it felt like to really be with God.

It was the beginning of a turning point in my life. Newton's Law of Motion states, "Every object persists in its state of rest or uniform motion in a straight line unless it is compelled to change that state by forces impressed on it." Camp was the force that changed my direction.

Although, camp provided me with peace and clarity, it was difficult to change all at once. Especially, not without a drastic push. I knew I'd changed, but I didn't realize how much. I still felt like it was possible to adjust my circumstances without necessarily making a clean break. There was a lot I still thought I could control.

At camp, it was especially hard to come to grips with reality because everyone seemed to have it all together. Everyone was happy. Everyone was just so in love with Jesus. Everyone was "living right." I was ashamed. Too ashamed to talk to anyone about what was really going on and I couldn't be free from something I couldn't talk about.

How could I tell people that I was living in sin? How could I tell them I enjoyed a lot of what I was in, but I was more than likely clinically depressed? How could I tell them I was struggling with a slightly physical, very emotionally abusive relationship?

With everything I had been through, the last thing I wanted was to be judged. So I spent the summer in a state of reflection. I avoided trips home on the weekend and tried to soak up as much peace as I could. I prayed, but mostly sat in silence. Looking back, I'm so grateful for that time. God could have bombarded me with scripture or persuasive words but He didn't. He knew exactly what I needed and that's what He did for me.

After summer camp, I was so refreshed, but it was difficult transitioning back home. Trying to keep peace while surrounded by darkness is tough. I had to find a way to take some of camp home with me. I started with the most important part of camp, which was rebuilding my relationship with God. Thankfully, an old friend introduced me to a new church and I was eager to go.

The church was an hour away from me, but the promoter had his car fixed, so I was free to get around. The first time I went, it was an amazing experience. I met my friend and his sister and we had a great time. When I left, I was so excited about the service, I forgot I had made plans to go to this guy's house. I felt like I shouldn't go. Something kept telling me not to, but I didn't want to keep blowing him off. He was a nice guy. He kept up with me at camp, texting me "good morning" every day. We had also hung out before, so I knew what to expect.

When I got to his house, we chilled on the couch. It was his mom's house and she was there, so I didn't feel any pressure to be intimate. I planned to work on my computer and kick it like we always did. It was harmless.

That's the night I woke up. When I realized I had somehow moved out of a space where I could control everything and I desperately was in need of saving. When I looked at my life and seriously asked myself, "How did I get here?"

Everything was normal. We laughed and joked. We even made out a little. Somehow, the topic of sex came up and I kind of thought it was a joke. His mother was upstairs so I didn't think he could be serious.

So he presented me with a playful ultimatum. He said he was going to go get the condom and if I was still there when he came back, we were going to have sex. I laughed. I had no intention of having sex with him, but I had still not actually used the word "no".

When he came back downstairs, I realized how serious he was. My playful tricks didn't work anymore. Laughter turned nervous, as we played tug of war for my pants and fear grew, paralyzing my body.

I never said no. The tug of war for my underwear was a shorter fight. I tried to resolve it in my mind. I never said no. Sex happened. I tried to engage, but I couldn't shake the thought that I didn't want it. I never wanted it.

When it was over, I got up and went to the bathroom. I tried so hard to reconcile the past few minutes in my head. I couldn't make my brain believe what had happened. As if admitting it made it real.

I sat on the toilet and looked down at my underwear. I saw blood. I wiped and saw more blood. I was broken. All of the justifications and explanations I was building in my mind for what happened were crushed at the sight of the bright red stain on my panties. I was nowhere near my period, but I was bleeding, which had never happened before and never happened again. It was all the proof I needed that it was real.

I broke down in tears in the bathroom, but I pulled myself together to get out of his house. I grabbed my stuff, told him I was leaving, and got in the car. I couldn't stop thinking how this was all my fault. I shouldn't have come. I got what I deserved. I never should have come.

I called my sisters that night and they were outraged. They asked me what I wanted to do, but I didn't want to do anything. What could I do? I never said "no".

I just never wanted to put myself in a situation like that again. In all honesty, I still can't say that he deserves to be crucified. I've never given written consent for sex before. It just naturally flowed. It was never like that. I blamed myself for not saying "no". Right or wrong, that's the burden I carried.

It was my wakeup call. That wasn't the life I wanted to live anymore. Somewhere along the way, I lost myself and I needed to get back.

THE CHILD ONCE LOST

"Once you've experienced being lost, you have a better sense of how important is it to know who you are and how important it is to never let that go."

When I finally recognized that I was lost, I didn't want that for myself. When you make changes in your life because you want to do something different, that's one thing. Usually, there's a hope that your life will be better than what it was. When you make one bad decision and your life changes drastically, that's another. I didn't make a decision to have a better life. I just made a dumb decision. Followed by other dumb decisions that got me to a place that I wasn't remotely close to who I was when I started.

My whole focus had to change. All I could think about was how much I wanted to be me again. I wanted to look in the mirror and not see some sad person who was stuck in this terrible place. I began to brainstorm about how to rediscover myself. How could I truly find myself again?

It was a life-changing thought. I was dumbfounded by the idea that I had somehow been wandering the world aimlessly and had no idea I was doing it. Part of me wanted to get back to who I was. Yet, I knew after all I had been through, I would never be that girl again. I really struggled with whether that was a good or bad thing.

Maybe the girl I lost was worth losing. Maybe the girl I would find is who I needed to be all along. Loving who I was felt like buying into a lie that I didn't need change when I knew that wasn't true. I had issues and I needed to work through them. Yet, completely hating who I had become was counterproductive to a point. I learned so much about myself and about the world around me. I needed to process through what to keep and what to re-imagine. I needed to make the old me and the new me, one person.

I felt as if I had a blank slate before me. I was granted an opportunity to learn from my mistakes. I had the ability to assess my life, make a plan, and commit to move forward.

I can't quite remember where the idea of blogging came from, but I do know it was something I always wanted to do. I could never seem to commit to it, though. I've always been an emotional writer, but putting those thoughts in a public space was a whole different ballgame. It was like having my diary broadcasted to the world.

That was a very intimidating idea for me. I've always been a very private person. Yet, my sole purpose for making the blog public was that I needed accountability. I needed people to challenge me. I needed to take a bold step that would push me forward and not back into the shadows. Writing alone was therapeutic, but if I made myself promises and no one knew, they would be much easier to break.

Once I settled on the blog as my form of accountability, I had to decide what my process would look like. That's where Elizabeth Gilbert came in. Fortunately for me, when I was deciding to go on a journey to rediscover myself, the book, Eat, Pray, Love, was made into a movie. Although, I didn't see the movie or read the book, I was inspired by the idea of a woman on a journey to self-discovery.

From the little that I knew about the actual story, I developed my own thoughts on what those things could look like in my life. I wanted to commit to an open journey of re-discovery, in which I would blog once a month about my progress. It was very dramatic but fun, and made the process easier for me to commit to.

As me and the promoter's lease was coming to an end, we had an opportunity to temporarily move in with my family. It seemed like a recipe for disaster, but it was perfect for where I was emotionally. It was safe and I needed a break from the instability I had become accustomed to.

It was difficult deciding between my peace and the fictional reality I had created. I knew that living with my family would reveal more about my relationship than I was comfortable revealing. At the same time, I desperately wanted to be free and I needed some place safe to get there.

I knew what I was attempting to do would be difficult. Although, I didn't want to admit it, making a decision to change was making a decision to leave him. I told myself that it was possible to move forward together, but the reality was that we were never supposed to be together in the first place. I made a commitment to be something to him that I was never meant to be – his savior. Living with my family allowed us to have space to see that.

Once our living situation was resolved, I prepared for my journey. In order to make sure I could actually write a blog a month, I started a month before the New Year. I made a yearlong commitment and needed a head start to prove to myself I could do it.

The original name of my blog was, "The Lost Child," where I publicly committed to "eat, pray, and love" for one full year. "Eat" represented indulging in things that I enjoyed. I committed to drawing, painting, laughing, eating, and just having fun, but in a way that was building and not self-destructive.

"Pray" represented my commitment to reconnect with God, although, I tried to avoid doing so in the traditional sense. I didn't want to focus just on "good deeds". I felt like that's where I went wrong in the first place. I wanted to develop a relationship with God that wouldn't end the way the last one did. A relationship, not as dependent upon rules, but on who I was and who God was and who we were in relationship together. I was committing to making a real effort to fall in love with God.

My last commitment was to "love" myself. That was something I'd never had to intentionally do before. I always accepted myself for who I was, but I don't think I was ever madly in love with that person. I feel like that's what made it easier to lose myself. I didn't want to expect someone else to be in love with someone I couldn't stand to be alone with.

I had to commit to putting myself first, which is something I'm not sure is completely "holy" from a churchy sense. I felt like I needed to take my life back and in order to do that, I couldn't worry about the promoter or any other man, or my friends, or whoever. I had to worry about myself, which translated into not getting into a relationship.

Not loving myself made me incapable of loving God or anyone else. The Bible talks about the greatest commandment being to love God and love your neighbor as you love yourself. Yet, I never realized that the Scripture identifies loving yourself as a standard for loving others. So, if you don't love you, you can't possibly love someone else.

In all of these internal processes, I noticed that my life was starting to shift. I was doing well in school, working, and overall, in a better state of being. I was also learning a lot professionally. I had an internship that granted me lots of experience with non-profit management, with a supervisor who had managed her non-profit for over twenty-five years.

As all of these things started to change, it was easier to see things for what they were. The promoter and I were in two completely different places in life. Although we still technically lived together, we were both dealing with life in very different ways.

I didn't have the time or energy to sacrifice anymore. I was done being a "good" friend/significant other/business partner. I was starting to prepare him for when I would no longer be there and it was hard.

When he got frustrated about something, it was difficult for me to engage him. I didn't have the same level of investment. I started to consider my needs over his. In sum, I lost interest in being miserable for his happiness.

It's hard to really understand where he was at that time emotionally. I wanted to believe he cared about me, but nothing really substantiated that claim.

He had a long list of admirers. Some helped with his business and others he engaged in a more intimate way. I became more of an advisor in a business sense and we began drifting. I, once again, saw him like I did when I first met him, but I was so much different.

As we grew apart, I became more and more frustrated with being alone. Part of my commitment to loving myself was to not commit to a serious relationship, but my heart still longed for one. I spent a lot of time processing my feelings about love, or the lack thereof, in my blog.

One post was centered on my ten "must-haves" in a man. It was filled with all the things I felt were lacking in the past two years. My list included the ability to love, loyalty, communication, compassion, flexibility, attractiveness, intelligence, humor, ambition, and a relationship with God. I ended the blog with asking, "Does this man exist?"

Around February or March, I was contacted by one of the guy counselors from the Christian camp I worked at. We'd worked together twice at camp, which meant that I met him sometime in 2008, but I didn't know him very well.

From what I did know through working together and our brief conversations over the years, was that he was a "nice guy". He'd dated a girl at camp for a long time and they'd recently ended their relationship. So, I grouped him in the "friend zone," nice guy group.

We exchanged numbers and planned to hang out, but my life was still very much all over the place. I was in school, working, and had an internship. Hang-outs were hard to come by those days. It also didn't help that the promoter and I were still living together, sharing a car, and I was in the re-discovery process. I had a lot going on.

Sometime in early April, he asked me to hang out again and I finally said yes. I remember thinking that I could not tell this man "no." Not again.

It was late. I was just getting off of work, but we made arrangements to go to Waffle House and talk. I went home to change and left the car for the promoter. I told him I was going to hang out with a friend and he looked at me suspiciously. Unbothered, I left with no more details. Besides the fact that the promoter and I had been through this already, I was legitimately going out to catch up with a friend.

Somehow a late night breakfast became a very significant moment in my life. It seemed like we talked about everything – from his break-up to some of our bad decisions we'd made over the past year, to camp life – and we laughed. I'm not sure we ever stopped laughing. It felt like the world stood still.

When he took me home, I felt like I'd been hit by some light, fluffy, warm thing. Even though, I was positive he had no intention of being anything more than friends. I wanted to be friends, but I was feeling something else. My mind was absolutely consumed by our time together.

In the morning, I was still thinking about it. It was insane. I remember pleading to God in the shower. I couldn't like him. It wasn't a part of the plan. I desperately needed the next man I dated to be my husband. I was tired of the hit and misses. Tired of falling for the "wrong" one. I knew he wasn't the one and I wasn't going to fall for him. He was a nice guy. A friend and that's all I wanted him to be.

I felt like God and I had an understanding when I left the shower. So, I was committed to making sure our relationship stayed exactly the way it was. Nothing more and nothing less.

My friend and I talked every day after that night. It was a very refreshing experience. Technically, I had known him for some time, but never really knew him. At camp, I remember thinking that he was strangely quiet and pretty intense. Now, it was like what I had imagined I would feel meeting my soul mate. We just became instant friends and I literally waited for moments to be around him. It was unreal.

As our friendship grew, my feelings grew more and more confusing. I wanted desperately not to feel anything romantic for him, but I couldn't help myself. I was falling for him. And it was the worst possible timing. He was perfect for me, at least who I would be, if I could get my life together. I was a complete mess.

One day, we were hanging out and I started to tell him about this guy I was considering dating. At first he seemed intrigued, yet as my story progressed, he became more and more solemn. After listening to me talk for a few minutes, he asked me a simple question, "Do you like him?"

Although the question was technically simple, it was very difficult to answer. I started by describing how dependable the other guy was and how much he liked me, but the more I explained, the more my friend pushed the question. The simple answer was no. I didn't like the other guy. I just didn't want to be alone anymore.

He said, "Don't do it." Without hesitation, he told me that I shouldn't be in a relationship with someone that I didn't like. This wasn't the first time I went to a guy friend for advice, but it was the first time that I listened without much resistance.

Don't get me wrong – I did try to come up with excuses. It's just that in most cases, regardless of the counter-argument, I did what I wanted to anyway. When I left that night, I was convinced of two things. One was that he was an amazing friend and two – I didn't need to date that other guy.

The next day, I talked to Za about our conversation and she had all the confirmation she needed to support that my friend had a thing for me. Although, I still wasn't convinced, it didn't take long for me to be proven wrong.

As Za and I were still talking, I got a text from him asking, "When are we going to go on a date?" My jaw dropped. Apparently, my friend did have a thing for me. Who knew?

Za was not opposed to an "I told you so," which I had to accept, after adamantly arguing that there was no way in the world he could like me. But it was still hard to accept.

I replied, "Why would we do that?"

"Because I think I'm starting to like you," he responded. To which I replied, "Really, why?" Of course, this was after Za urged me not to.

He took a little while to respond before texting back. But when he did, he explained all of the things he saw in me that he liked. It was a nice change of pace. So, I agreed to the date.

Later that week, we went to dinner and a movie. On the one hand, it was very familiar. Conversation was easy. We laughed and really enjoyed ourselves. On the other hand, expectations had changed. It was no longer two friends hanging out. I was in a place I hadn't navigated in a while. I was officially opening myself up to someone and I had no idea what to expect.

My life was still in pieces and my silly heart was hoping for love once again. The promoter was still living downstairs in the basement. I was still struggling with emotional issues. I didn't see how it was possible to even consider "like", let alone a relationship, at that point in my life.

I remember one night, before our "first date," we were hanging out at one of my grad school cohort's apartments and I was swearing off all men. I went on a complete rant about how terrible men were and how stupid women were. I think my exact words were "Good men do not exist." I had no regard for the fact that he sat there across from me, listening to me tear his entire gender to pieces.

Later that night, I got a text saying, "I want to be a good guy." I was devastated. All I could do was run back the last few hours in my mind and try to imagine how it must have felt to sit there and listen to that. Most guys would have argued with me, but in the moment, he was reflective. It made me feel terrible.

After our first date, with everything out on the table, I had to figure out if this was something I really wanted. I had to figure out if this was something I was even capable of giving a real try. There was something very different about this time, whether it was where I was or who he was, it was an encounter like no other.

If I was going to even attempt to move forward with him, I had to let go of so much. Things I had grown so used to carrying around with me. I had to shed pain, fear, insecurity, defeat, hopelessness, depression, and most importantly – the promoter.

At this point, I didn't know what else to do other than take it to God. I said, "Okay God, I already shared how I didn't want to like this guy and somehow we're here. My only resolve is to be open with him. I need you to make this decision easy for me."

My plan was to tell my friend everything and if he still wanted to be with me, we would have to take it day by day. Everything inside of me was in knots on the day we were supposed to talk. I feared he would listen intently, ask a few questions and run as fast as he could.

He didn't know how broken I was. No one did. He didn't know everything I'd done in the name of my sanity, or that I was living with someone. Yet, somehow I felt like he could see me. In all that I had been through, even when I couldn't see myself, he made me feel alive again.

Although it was a difficult decision to share where I had been with someone who could have easily walked away, I knew I had to. I needed to be free. I knew at that moment that the man I needed was going to have to be strong enough to walk all of this out with me.

On the day I decided to confess all my sins, I came home from school and the promoter and I got into it. We were preparing to move into a new space as roommates and he told me that he didn't want the cat to come with us. Being over our situation and burdened with how to talk to my friend about moving forward, I wasn't in the mood.

I took care of the cat; I didn't want to get rid of her. He told me that we were getting rid of the cat and that was it. I told him we were not and it turned into what all of our arguments did – an over-reaction.

He got so upset with me, he went upstairs, took the cat out of my room and locked himself and the cat downstairs in the basement. Frustrated and in tears, I took a seat at the dining room table. My computer was open and when I went to use it, I saw that his Facebook messenger was up with a conversation between him and the young chick from Miami. I proceeded to read through the conversation and the majority of it wasn't new information.

He was coaching her on the conversation she and I were supposed to have a few months back. He had a long list of what she could and could not share. Most of what he didn't want her to say was irrelevant. I could have cared less about the inner workings of their relationship and there was a lot that I had already assumed.

Yet, as I read, I felt a nervous tension growing. It was a question I had for quite some time. Something that I made clear was a deal-breaker for me and he swore, he never did and never would do. After all of the Do's and Don'ts, he instructed her not to tell me that they had sex in my car.

I remember freezing, re-reading, and then trying to breathe, but I couldn't. So I re-read it over and over, hoping the words would somehow transform on my screen. I could feel the rage swell in my fingertips, run up through my arms, creep into my heart and shoot back through the rest of my body. I can't tell you whether I actually saw red, or whether it was a figment of my imagination. I just knew I had no control over what happened next.

I dashed from the table, frantically searching for something to unlock the basement door. After using a kitchen knife to unlock the basement door, I flew downstairs and jumped on him.

I don't remember seeing anything. I just remember throwing punches in a frenzy, scratching and pulling whatever I could get my hands on. I kept saying, "The one thing I asked you not to do! You had sex with her in MY CAR?"

I was like a broken record. He just tried to protect himself, but he was too caught off guard to react. I snapped. I wanted so badly to physically hurt him like he had been breaking my heart over and over again.

When I finally stopped, all I could tell him was that he needed to get out of my face. He needed to leave or I was going to kill him. He'd done the one thing I felt was completely unforgivable. My car was my only place of solitude on so many occasions and he just couldn't respect me enough to leave that one space for me.

I went upstairs to cool off. It only took thirty minutes for him to pack and get picked up. When he walked out of the door, I remember locking the door and thinking, "Wow, that's it." That's all it took.

I sat for a while, trying to process. "Is he really gone?"

When I was screaming and telling him to leave, I wasn't thinking I was kicking him out. I was thinking that he had to get out of my face because I couldn't control myself. I wanted to hurt him, but I didn't realize he could get up and leave that easily.

Somehow, I trapped myself in this place where I was convinced he couldn't survive without me. But he was a grown man and on top of that, he was surviving long before me and would be surviving long after.

I texted my friend and told him I would probably have to cancel our plans to meet up. He asked why, of course, and I told him that it was a long story, but I had just gotten into a fight and I needed time. He told me he was on his way and I said okay.

He picked me up and we sat in his car in a store parking lot. I told him everything. I was so afraid of what he would think. I remember looking over to him and asking him how he felt after I shared my tragic life story. I don't know what I expected him to say. I just assumed no man would want to put up with all that. At least not for some girl he was barely emotionally invested in.

He paused and said, "He's gone, right?"

I said, "Yeah." He said, "Ok, cool." My life went from overly complicated to extremely simplified in an instant.

We made no commitments that night. There was only an understanding. Both of us were interested in pursuing something more – whatever that meant – and that was good enough for us. That was the night of our very first kiss.

I wish I could say that was the end of my journey. The promoter left, I fell in love and we lived happily ever after, but there was a lot to unpack in the days to come. I was in recovery for some time after that night. I was still rebuilding from being completely broken. So much so, I really had to rely on God to see me through. In order to truly be together, we had several hurdles to cross.

One major hurdle was that I needed to talk to his ex-girlfriend. I have always been of the model, that you do not talk to a friend's ex. Even when it came to my friends voicing that they were attracted to someone that made them automatically unavailable. I never wanted to deal with any complications that could come from dating someone's ex.

So I had to talk to her. I couldn't even think of moving forward without talking to her. I think coming out of my situation made me even more sensitive to consider the feelings of other women around me. I didn't want to be unintentional anymore.

This was something that was difficult for my friend to understand. For him, he didn't need to ask his ex-girlfriend for permission and I agreed. That wasn't really the point. The point was, she and I needed to have a difficult, but honest conversation in order for me to move forward with a clear conscience.

I remember being so nervous. I was nervous about what she would think of me. What she would think of us? It was hard. She and I weren't technically friends, but I did know her well enough to have this conversation. She was a good person and she deserved to hear it from me first.

When I reached out to talk, she was warm and friendly, as always. We shared formalities, while I worked up the courage to share something I hoped wouldn't have any effect on her – knowing it most likely would.

I sat at my desk, not breathing, and waiting for the moment I would have to share why I reached out. Choosing my words as carefully as possible, I told her that my friend and I had been spending time together. I told her that I was beginning to really like him, which was my reason for calling.

It was tough. There were no tears. I could just tell she was processing and had a few follow-up questions, which we talked through gracefully. When it was over, I left the conversation feeling free to make a decision on whether we could really give us a shot.

I also left the conversation feeling better about honor among women. While being with the promoter, I often wondered why women were so comfortable dishonoring each other. I had felt so disrespected on many occasions and I couldn't figure out why it seemed like such a normal thing for women. There is an obvious "bro code," yet women seem to have little to no rules concerning how we operate.

I get it. It's difficult. Yet, considering her, at least for me, was therapeutic for me too. I gave her what I felt I deserved in the past and hoped that in the future that same consideration would be returned to me.

Once my friend and I established that we were going to give "whatever" a try, we had to deal with the giant jackrabbit in the room: Lust. Now that I started it was really difficult to not engage with someone I really liked.

Needless to say, we didn't abstain from sex. Although, as time grew, our desire to work at it became greater, it was a major challenge for us. We knew we had something special, so we didn't want our relationship to be defined by blind passion.

For me, I didn't "need" sex, as much as it was a habit. In addition, sex made me feel powerful. It was still my means of controlling the situation. And although it was a challenge for both of us, he was the stronger of the two of us.

This led to having to deal with feelings of rejection and attempting to manage my desires for sex even outside of our relationship. The stronger he was in saying "no," the more difficult it was for me to believe he desired me. Which also created an issue of me wanting to gain control in the same ways I did while with the promoter.

So, we kept the discussion open. I shared with him how I was feeling and he respected my process to grow in that area. It was amazing. Telling someone who meant the world to me that I was struggling to stay faithful and him responding with love and understanding was life-changing.

I knew I was no longer lost when I developed truth to combat the lies that were planted in my mind. I accepted that the good and bad things that happened in my life took a team effort. God is an amazing God that wants the best for me, but I have to play a major role in that as well.

I had to accept that no one choice, good or bad, ultimately defined me. I had to play an active role in defining who I was and who I wanted to be over time. My actions are a reflection of the space I am in, not who I am. I am who I want, strive, and succeed or fail at being every day for the rest of my life.

Today I am a wife, mother, friend, daughter, and writer. I am a woman who has a story to tell and a woman who strives to be more like and as close to Jesus as she can get. Most importantly, I know who I am and I actively and fluidly participate in building and dismantling that woman every day to be a more improved model of myself.

REFLECTIONS

As I reflect on this journey I took to write this book, I can only credit God for getting me here. Recently, Za asked me how I was coming along with the final edits and I sighed deeply, disappointed at how close I'd been for so long.

I am not a personal believer in telling your business to the world. I've always been a private person. I've always felt that people judge what they think they understand about you and the less you give people, the less they can understand. Unfortunately, the challenge with this thinking is that it's selfish.

When Tyreke preached the message on the power of your testimony, I cringed. "Who can get anything from my story?"

His message was so clear: your story can have a life-changing effect on the person sitting next to you, waiting to hear, "Girl, I've been there before" or "I thought I was alone."

Even still, this was very difficult for me to write. You wouldn't believe the amount of affirmation I had to receive to get through this. Somehow, at every moment when I let my story slip into a distant memory, my soldiers would push and say, "You're not done yet."

I've had to fight for this.

And I say all this to say that I would have been the first person to tell you to keep your story to yourself. Now, I will be the first person to tell you that your story needs to be told.

Not many people have read this as I write, but when I told people what I was setting out to do, they've stood with me. They encouraged me. They've told me how much it needed to be done. God is all over this journey.

In my entire process of re-discovery and "becoming found," I didn't realize that my true healing would come from putting my heart on a couple of page. My scars, my dirty little secrets, my life. I never knew how easy it was to be held captive by the secrets I kept.

When I was a freshman in college, I had a dream that I was climbing a mountain. I'm not sure who was with me, but I know it was a man and when we got to the top, I jumped.

When I landed, I was in a bed of dandelions that were leafless and ready to be blown for wishes. It was beautiful.

I began spinning and spinning, as the white feathers carrying seeds spun all around me. It was breathtaking. At some point in my spinning, I became overwhelmed. I was overwhelmed to the point I couldn't breathe. So I stopped abruptly and all the seeds fell.

I paused for a second and resumed spinning until I became overwhelmed again. Yet, this time it didn't seem like I could stop. My vision went black for a split second and there was a man standing before me. It was snowing, still and quiet. We were all dressed up and he was standing before me smiling. We left that place together.

I will forever hold in my heart that this was a dream about my friend and now husband. When I had this dream, I thought the dandelions symbolized how I can often take on more than I can bear. Then I want to run and hide to regroup. I thought this man might help me find peace in those times.

Now, I believe the dream was foretelling what would bring me to him. It symbolized how I would find myself overwhelmed by life, lost, and that's where he'd find me. That's where he would accept me in my mess and that's where we would begin our journey together.

I say that to say, no matter where you are in life, God is always so many steps ahead. God wanted the best for me and in my darkest hour, He was there waiting to bless me.

My husband and I are not perfect, by any means. Yet, he is the most perfect man for me. I don't know what that means for our future. I just know that as I look through my story, God has always made provisions and he was one of them.

Through this journey, I've realized that I have to recognize those things that God has blessed me with and the things He hasn't. Understanding what God has placed in my life changes my source of strength for sustaining it. I believe God provides me with a special strength to address issues in my marriage, whereas in my previous relationships, I tried to sustain it on my own and it was a disaster.

I don't think believers understand that you can operate out of your own strength, in the same way unbelievers don't understand how different life is with God. Again, it's a partnership. It's a relationship that is cultivated through our experiences with Christ, Who teaches us what it means to stand by someone in their darkest hour, yet, love them just the same.

My journey has taught me that sometimes getting over something means facing it head on. Writing the second part of this book was transformative. Trying to remember how it felt to be lost made me have to face the reality of what happened in those times. It also forced me accept the blame for the parts of my downfall that I was responsible for.

I had to find the reason why I went through the things I did and face the fact that the majority of it was me. I chose a path that I didn't have to take.

Sometimes, I feel like we spend so much time blaming others, we never find the real issue is our own choices. Our own stubbornness. Our lives are filled with excuses, "Well, my mom," or "My father always disappointed me," or "He left me broken." Yet, we can never find healing because the answer is not in those people.

I am in no way saying that these things don't matter, nor am I saying that everything that happens to us is our fault. What I am saying is that when we start to take ownership for our role in our circumstances, only then will we understand how to move forward.

After all of the darkness I've experienced, my life is so vastly different. My husband and I got back into youth ministry and we built relationships with friends who encourage and build us up. These are also the same friends who tell us when we are wrong.

We stepped out on faith and chosen to pursue our passions which has been challenging, but amazingly fulfilling. If I've learned anything from this experience, I've learned that I never want to be lost again. I never want to be without God again. I never want to be without me again.

I've also learned that who I believe I am and the decisions I make in response to that understanding is essential in moving forward. I can never let myself go to a place like that again. Not knowing what I know now.

www.ingramcontent.com/pod-product-compliance
Lightning Source LLC
Chambersburg PA
CBHW051649040426
42446CB00009B/1052